# THE MARTIAL ARTS INSTRUCTOR'S TOOLBOX

## by Dave Kovar

# The Martial Arts Instructor's Toolbox

Copyright © 2012 by Dave Kovar

Design by: Kyle Archer

www.kovarsystems.com

Printed in U.S.A

Dedicated To My Fellow Martial Arts Instructors

# TABLE OF CONTENTS

TO MY FELLOW MARTIAL ARTS INSTRUCTORS:

In just a few short decades, Martial Arts has traveled from being an obscure, cult-like obsession of just a few to a mainstream, worldwide phenomenon. No longer is it confined to dirty town halls or stuffy basements. There are world-class training facilities in virtually every city on the globe.

What is responsible for the explosive growth in popularity of Martial Arts? There is a growing understanding that Martial Arts goes way beyond mere self-defense or fitness... that it has something to offer everyone regardless of age or gender.

What challenges face modern civilization? Obesity, violence, low self-esteem, lack of confidence, questionable morals and peer pressure, to name a few. Martial Arts taught right addresses each of these problems and more.

I'll never forget my first chance at teaching Martial Arts. I was a 14-year-old blue belt with less than a year's experience. Instructor Bill, one of the instructors at the karate school I attended, didn't show up to teach his set of private lessons. The owner of the school and my instructor, Sensei Bruce, called Bill to see if he was coming in. I could tell by the look on Sensei Bruce's face that Bill wasn't going to make it in that day. Then he looked in my direction. I could tell he was weighing the pros and cons of either canceling Bill's lessons or having me teach his classes.

The next thing I know, I'm giving a private lesson to an adult man in his thirties. Scared to death, I did my best imitation of Sensei Bruce and imparted as much knowledge as a 14-year-old blue belt could. From forgetting the bow to mixing up the footwork in the kata we were reviewing (and I forgot his name), I failed miserably. However, this experience lit a fire in my belly. I then knew exactly what I wanted to do, teach Martial Arts. And I knew that I wanted to be good at it! In those days, there was no formal instructor training. Learning how to teach was all on-the-job.

I proceeded to teach part-time through high school. In November of 1978, about six months after graduation, I found myself running my own Martial Arts school. I still had had no formal training in how to teach. Everything I did while teaching a class I either made up or copied from someone else. When it came time to look for assistant instructors to help me in class, I knew there had to be a better way to learn. So I started a semi-formal instructors' training program. We met once a week to discuss teaching techniques and concepts. I honestly can't remember what we did during that hour except that we focused on making sure everyone knew the moves well enough to teach them. Nevertheless, the seed to of *The Martial Arts Instructor's Toolbox* was planted.

About a decade later, I brought my older brother Tim into the business to be my partner. He brought with him a lot of formal education and real-world experience. Our small school took off. Business was good and it soon became apparent that we needed more instructors.

Tim was adamant that we formalize our instructor training program. He also felt that we should emphasize more than just teaching proper techniques. This made complete sense to me and the two of us began working on a formal instructors training program. And we've never stopped refining our program.

In 1994, we produced and distributed a video series called How to teach Martial Arts to Children. In 1997, we launched a formal Martial Arts instructors program for the industry called Martial Arts Career Training (or the MACT Manual). We sold thousands of videos and manuals over the next few years and I'm proud to say that many of the top schools in the country still use them for staff training.

One of main reasons why our How to Teach series and the MACT Manual were so effective is that they placed a strong emphasis on the importance of an instructor's attitude towards teaching, as well as on specific teaching techniques and strategies.

Although I'm proud of our former products, we've learned a lot about teaching since then. *The Martial Arts Instructor's Toolbox* is the culmination of all we've learned so far. Hopefully, it will prove to be a great review for senior instructors, as well as an excellent foundation for new teachers.

Happy teaching!


Dave Kovar

# THE SIMPLE TRUTH

BUSHIDO

MODERN-DAY SAMURAI

SERVICE

GOOD BUSINESS

PASSION

COMMITMENT

SYSTEMATIC APPROACH

INTRODUCTION

*The key to our long-term success as an industry*
*lies in our ability to focus on improving other people's lives.*
*The challenge for Martial Arts instructors is to find a system*
*that will allow them to put this truth into action in every*
*aspect of their school and on a sustained basis.*
*This is why I wrote 'The Martial Arts Instructor's Toolbox .'*

—*Dave Kovar*

## THE SUCCESS OF THE MARTIAL ARTS INDUSTRY

People often speculate about the future of our industry. Have we reached our prime? Are we past our prime? Or are we still growing? The answer depends upon the way that we, as an industry, run our schools today and tomorrow.

## PUTTING FIRST THINGS FIRST

If the majority of schools decide to improve upon the existing good reputation we have created so far, then the sky is the limit! We just have to remember to put the students before the money and the money will follow. This concept is not new, nor is it controversial. The challenge for many instructors is to find a system or approach to keep this truth in sight and put it into action in every detail of their schools.

## THE RIGHT PEOPLE

The only way to do good business is to do good business. Because we are in the business of teaching Martial Arts, the most vital element to the success of our business is employing high-quality, passionate instructors who are committed to helping to improve people's lives. Once you have that covered, you can concentrate on the details of running the business.

## PRIORITIES FOR SUCCESS

The location and cleanliness of your school, advertising and marketing, bookkeeping and phones skills are all extremely important elements and have to be superior in order for your business to thrive. But remember, for long-term success, be a Martial Artist first, a teacher second and a businessperson third.

> *Be a Martial Artist first, a teacher second,*
> *and a businessperson third.*

## BE A MARTIAL ARTIST FIRST

Martial Arts as we know it today has its roots in bushido, the code of the Samurai. Samurai means to serve and the best Samurai did not take their position lightly. They held themselves to the highest standard in all aspects of their lives.

Because they were warriors, they continually honed their Martial Arts skills and fitness levels, as these literally meant the difference between life and death. Perfect health was their goal, so they lived their lives accordingly. Samurai were highly aware of how the effect their environment and habits of consumption affected them.

Most importantly, the best Samurai lived a life of service. They gave to their communities and were noble examples of human potential. Here are a few traditional Samurai phrases that are as relevant to today's Martial Artist as they were the first time they were spoken:

**Bushi-ni-nihon-nashi.** No two words; don't speak with forked tongue. In modern times, we call this living with integrity.

**Hou' shi Sei-shin.** Spirit of contribution. Being service-minded.

**Chou you de ari.** Moderation, variety and balance.

**Gan batte kuda sai.** Always doing your best.

*Commit to living the life of a modern-day Samurai.*

## BE A TEACHER SECOND

Is there a better way to live a life of service than teaching? What is more rewarding than giving the gift of what you have learned and discovered over many years to others? The best teachers teach by example. By being a Martial Artist first, your job as a teacher is already half done.

*Excellent teachers do their best to live up to the Instructors' Creed:*

*I will teach this class because it is the most important class I will ever teach.*

*I am patient and enthusiastic.*

*I lead by example.*

Many old-school instructors were of the mindset that their students were lucky to have them as a teacher. The more empowering (and effective) mindset for the Martial Arts instructor is to appreciate your students for, without your students, you can't be a teacher. Sincerely believe in your students' potential and make their needs a high priority.

Another outdated paradigm that many instructors still hold onto is the extremely passive approach of assuming that a student enrolled in their program will train successfully and someday be a black belt. But reality paints us a completely different picture. Most students who enroll in a Martial Arts program quit (and usually quite quickly), *unless we intervene with superior student service.*

- How can we provide superior student service? Ask yourself these powerful questions:

- What can I do today to ensure that my students will come back to their next class?

- What can I do today to ensure that my students have the best possible class and will return for one more?

- What can I do today to ensure that my students' parents will bring them back to class one more time?

- What can I do today to ensure that my students leave class thinking, "I'm glad I came"?

- What can I do today to ensure that my students like how they feel about themselves when they are at my Martial Arts school?

*Asking these questions is the first step to providing superior student service. The real key, however, is taking action on your answers. Most likely, whichever question you ask, the answer will involve teaching a great Martial Arts class.*

## BE A BUSINESSPERSON THIRD

You are already well on your way to success if you're a Martial Artist first and a teacher second. To be a successful businessperson is to have a systematic approach for retention and ethical referrals, a structured and consistent approach or strategy to teaching so that you maximize the impact of each class, and a vital curriculum designed to improve the lives of your students—all things *The Martial Arts Instructor's Toolbox* provides.

# THE MINDSET OF A MARTIAL ARTS INSTRUCTOR

SIMPLICITY

FRIENDLINESS

CLEANLINESS

GREAT CLASSES

EXCELLENT COMMUNICATION

COMMITMENT

POSITIVE RECRUITMENT

CHAPTER 1

You can't lose with the following five mindsets!

1. We are the friendliest place in town.

2. We are the cleanest place in town.

3. We only teach GREAT classes, never just good classes.

4. We are excellent at student/parent communication.

5. We look for opportunities to recruit new students every day.

## KEEP IT SIMPLE

During a visit to one of our Martial Arts academies, the school's manager—a great, hardworking, ethical guy—explained how he had been working on this sophisticated formula to track students' progress and attendance. He felt like he was onto something, but there were a lot of moving parts and it would be some time before he had it all figured out.

"Too complicated," I thought. And then I remembered a story once told to me. There once was a famous landscape architect, a Master, who traveled the world creating amazing gardens and landscapes at prestigious locations. People reported that, whenever he felt particularly challenged, he'd pull out a piece of paper from his pocket, look at it, nod, fold it back up, and then get to work creating another masterpiece. People were astounded by the brilliant designs that would seem to come out of nowhere after he studied that tiny piece of paper.

Eventually this master designer died. His colleagues approached his widow and asked to see that mysterious piece of paper. After much to-do, she allowed them one glance at the old slip of paper. They gathered around her as she unfolded it.

"When laying sod, always put the green side up."

So, the next time your find yourself in over your head and not sure of which way to turn, remember, "When laying sod, always put the green side up." In other words, keep it simple; don't overcomplicate things; and get back to basics.

> *I love this story because it reminds me that so often we manage to over-complicate our lives, our careers, and our relationships.*

For example, Martial Arts school operators tend to get easily sidetracked by the latest trend or the newest ad. They forget to keep it simple and stick with the Five Vital Mindsets.

## VITAL MINDSET #1: WE ARE THE FRIENDLIEST PLACE IN TOWN.

In Malcolm Gladwell's book, *Blink*, he describes the importance of first impressions. He explains that research shows that most people make up their mind about a person, situation or organization very quickly (within the first few seconds). Can someone get a great first impression of your school and not enroll? Yes. Can someone have a terrible first impression of your school and still enroll? Yes. But generally speaking, people make their decisions very quickly after entering your school. And if they get a good first impression, they are more likely to enroll. With this in mind, one of the most important things that we can do to make an excellent first impression is to create a friendly environment. This begins with the highest-level instructor and it works its way down through the ranks. Remember that walking into a Martial Arts school for the first time can be incredibly intimidating. It takes a lot of courage. A friendly environment goes a long way to help put a potential student at ease, as well as retain the students already enrolled.

## VITAL MINDSET #2: WE ARE THE CLEANEST PLACE IN TOWN.

There are a lot of things you cannot control, but the cleanliness of your school is not one of them. Keeping your school impeccably clean projects professionalism and inspires confidence in your school. One time, a grandmother inquired about enrolling her grandson in our school. She explained how she had checked into the school down the street had decided against it. I knew the owner of the school—he was an excellent Martial Artist and a very good teacher—so I was curious to know why she had decided against the school. She had used the bathroom at the school and it was dirty. To her, a dirty bathroom meant a bad school. Cleanliness is everyone's job, not just the janitor's or school owner's.

## VITAL MINDSET #3: WE TEACH GREAT CLASSES, NEVER JUST GOOD CLASSES.

I teach best when my physical energy level is high and I'm super motivated to teach. The concept behind this mindset is to make a conscious effort to teach a GREAT class every This doesn't guarantee that every class is going to be great, but it dramatically stacks the odds in your favor.

## VITAL MINDSET #4: WE ARE EXCELLENT AT STUDENT/PARENT COMMUNICATION.

Student/parent communication tends to be the weakest point for most instructors and school owners. Over the years, I have had my fair share of challenges with students, parents and staff members. In retrospect, I can trace these challenges back to poor communication on my part. It's important to remember that the responsibility of communication is in the hands of the communicator and not the person with whom you are communicating. In other words, it's our responsibility as instructors to communicate well with our students and their parents.

Great communication is twofold. First, strive to be excellent at getting the word out about special events, class schedule changes, belt promotions, specific requirements that students need for the next rank, school closures due to weather, and other related issues. In fact, over-communicate. Secondly, develop the habit of giving students feedback about their progress on a regular basis. We should look for opportunities to compliment their improvement, as well as ways to help them improve.

VITAL MINDSET #5: WE LOOK FOR OPPORTUNITIES TO RECRUIT NEW STUDENTS EVERY DAY.

Everyone is responsible to help build your school. This responsibility does not belong solely to the Director of Marketing or to the Program Director. Every member of the team should be constantly seeking and seizing opportunities to promote the school.

## THE FIVE MINDSETS CHECKLIST

✓ We are the friendliest place in town.

✓ We are the cleanest place in town.

✓ We only teach great classes, never just good classes.

✓ We are excellent at Student/Parent communication.

✓ We spend some quality time on New Student Acquisition Strategies every day.

# THE INSTRUCTORS CREED

ENTHUSIASM

PATIENCE

LEADERSHIP

EXCITEMENT

Using *The Instructor's Creed* as a foundation for all your instruction will help you achieve long-term success. You can use The Instructor's Creed as a solid metric or standard to examine the situation when classes aren't going well, too.

## THE INSTRUCTOR'S CREED

1.  I will teach this class ~~as if~~ BECAUSE it is the most important class I'll ever teach.

2.  I am patient and enthusiastic.

3.  I lead by example.

## THE COMMON FACTOR OF ALL SUCCESSFUL MARTIAL ARTS SCHOOLS

Over the years, I have been able to visit hundreds of the top schools in the country and network with their owners. During these visits, I focus on the attributes that make them stand out as unique. While everyone does things a little differently, I did notice the top schools have at least one thing in common:

EXCITING AND DYNAMIC CLASSES TAUGHT BY ENTHUSIASTIC, WELL-TRAINED INSTRUCTORS!

More than twenty years ago, I developed The Instructor's Creed as an affirmation to say on my way to a particularly rough, off-campus class that

I dreaded teaching. Eventually, we had our staff memorize it. I still use it on a regular basis and have found it to be a great anchor for getting myself focused for the class at hand.

## INSTRUCTOR'S CREED #1: I WILL TEACH THIS CLASS AS IF IT WERE THE MOST IMPORTANT CLASS I'LL EVER TEACH.

There might be times when you are getting ready to line up a class and, due to the size of the class or a personal challenge you're preoccupied with, you aren't very motivated. Maybe you're tempted to just give teaching that class half an effort or decide you want to bow the class out early.

It is during times like these that I remind myself of The Instructor's Creed and actually say to myself, "I will teach this class as if it were the most important class I'll ever teach." Why? Because it is.

Every time your students come to class, they are either one step closer to getting their Black Belt or one step closer to quitting. And the instructor's performance will be the deciding factor.

I remind my instructors to approach a class with only one student with the same enthusiasm as they would a class of 30+ students, as it's the only way I know of to grow a class or keep the students they have. I remind my staff that, in the student's mind, the instructor is only as good as their last class with that instructor.

INSTRUCTOR'S CREED #2: I AM PATIENT AND ENTHUSIASTIC.

*Patience* and *Enthusiam* are the two most important qualities of any teacher.

> *Your students won't care how much you know until*
> *they know how much you care.*

Patience is one way of showing that you care. Being patient with your students allows your students to relax and feel comfortable, therefore making it much easier for them to learn.

Teaching with enthusiasm enables you to excite your students and hold their interest longer. It also makes you more interesting. Your students will be more interested if you are interesting!

INSTRUCTOR'S CREED #3: I LEAD BY EXAMPLE.

Walk your talk! Don't say one thing and do another. Live the exact life that you are telling your students to live. Only then will your students trust you and be receptive to any input you might give them.

> *"What you are speaks so loudly,*
> *I can't hear what you are saying."*
>
> —*Ralph Waldo Emerson*
>
> *"The three most important ways to lead people are:*
> *by example... by example... by example..."*
>
> —*Albert Schweitzer*

## THE INSTRUCTOR'S CREED CHECKLIST

✓ I will teach this class as if it was the most important class I'll ever teach.

✓ I was unwaveringly patient and enthusiastic.

✓ I am setting a good example for my students.

# 16 EFFECTIVE TEACHING TACTICS, TECHNIQUES, AND TOOLS

INTENTION

MINDFULNESS

HOSPITALITY

WARMTH

GLADNESS

POSITIVITY

RESPECT

SAFETY

PROFESSIONALISM

INFLUENCE

CHAPTER 3

The following 16 Tactics, Techniques and Tools work together seamlessly to form a solid base for every instructor who puts them to work.

1.  Be friendly on purpose.

2.  Use your Transformational Communication skills.

3.  Harness the power of Focus Anchors.

4.  Establish the habit of Positive Pre-framing.

5.  Habituate The 3x3 Rule.

6.  Praise publicly. Reprimand privately.

7.  Utilize the 3 D's: Demonstrate, Detail, and Drill.

8.  Practice Praise-Correct-Praise.

9.  Use influence instead of authority.

10. Always follow the Smiling-Sweating-Learning Rule (SSL).

11. Practice the art of Disguising Repetition.

12. Practice Zero Downtime.

13. Rise to the occasion when working with challenging students.

14. Make every Huddle Discussion a masterpiece.

15. Always stress Safety First.

16. Never compromise the instructor/student relationship.

## EVERYTHING WE DO, OR DON'T DO, MATTERS

Perhaps you have heard of the scientific hypothesis referred to as the butterfly effect? The butterfly effect refers to the idea that even the flapping of a butterfly's wings can create tiny changes in the atmosphere that will have big effects. The flapping wing represents a small change in the initial condition of the system, which can cause a chain of events leading to large-scale alterations of events (similar to the domino effect). Had the butterfly not flapped its wings, the trajectory of a specific situation might have been vastly different.

For example, the flapping of a butterfly's wings could ultimately alter the path of a tornado—or delay, accelerate, or even prevent the occurrence of a tornado. While the butterfly does not cause the tornado in the sense of providing the energy for the tornado, it does cause it in the sense that the flap of its wings is an essential part of the initial conditions that alters the outcome. Without that flap, that particular tornado would not have existed.

Our actions really do matter... all of them. Every decision we make, big and small, affects our future and the future of those with whom we share our world. That is a pretty big responsibility, isn't it? Yes, but it makes life simpler as well. (Bear in mind that I said simpler, not easier.)

Being mindfully aware that everything matters helps us to shape our decisions, both unconsciously and consciously. All we have to remember to do when we are faced with a challenge is to do what is right. Sometimes it seems hard to know what is right but, more often than not, we know.

And when we know what is right to do but don't do it, our inaction or wrong action can have an enormous impact or butterfly effect on everyone. So the next time you are faced with a difficult decision, don't seek the easiest or quickest solution or the solution that you feel most benefits you. Instead, focus on what is right and then give it your all and do it.

Remember, *Everything Matters*. The following 16 Incredibly Effective Teaching Tactics, Techniques and Tools are designed to help you have an exponentially positive impact on the lives of your students.

## INCREDIBLY EFFECTIVE TEACHING TACTIC #1: BE FRIENDLY ON PURPOSE.

Make people feel welcome. Have you ever walked into an establishment and felt like the person who was supposed to be helping you didn't care about you or your business? She may not have been mean or surly, but she certainly didn't make you feel like she was glad to see your or happy to serve you? This can happen within a business too, when we deal with our fellow instructors and others in our schools (our internal customers). The people we are supposed to support and serve within our own organization.

RULE OF 3

1. Be the first to say "Hello."

2. Smile.

3. Be sincerely interested in them.

> *Remember that your students have choices about where to spend their time and money—and who to hire as a Martial Arts instructor. Make the effort to put your best face forward when dealing with EVERYONE. Be friendly on purpose!*

ALWAYS...

Extend a sense of hospitality and warmth. Smile! Make eye contact! Shake hands if it's appropriate. Let your customers (internal or external) know you're very glad to see them.

Being friendly shows respect to those with whom you deal. People will continue to do business where they feel respected.

Try to be the first to say "Hello" or "Good Morning." If you can't help someone right away, let them know you'll be right with them.

Smile. Smile. Smile. This is so important! Remember to smile when you're on the phone, too—people can hear the smile in your voice!

Make appropriate eye contact to engage your customers and let them know you are listening and attentive to their needs.

*Remember not to take it personally if someone is not friendly back. Just do your best to be warm and helpful.*

INCREDIBLY EFFECTIVE TEACHING TACTIC #2: USE YOUR TRANS-FORMATIONAL COMMUNICATION SKILLS.

As we all know, we communicate with more than just our words. The tone of our voices and our body language often say MORE than our words! So it's vital that your body and voice are congruent with your message—this is Transformational Communication.

RULE OF 3

1. Tonality.

2. Physiology.

3. Physiognomy.

*And if your Voice Tone and Body Language do not match your words, guess what? Transformational Communication always trumps words. People hear and believe it over your words.*

ALWAYS...

Make sure that your tonality, physiology and physiognomy match your intent and objective to help ensure clear communication and desired outcomes.

## TONALITY, PHYSIOLOGY AND PHYSIOGNOMY

**Tonality**. This is the tone and pitch of your voice. The volume and speed at which you speak will affect the way your message is received.

**Physiology**. This is body language. Your gestures, movements and mannerisms can tell a story that either goes with or conflicts with the idea you are trying to convey.

**Physiognomy**. This is the language of your face. Your facial expression declares the truth of your feelings when you are communicating with someone in person.

## INCREDIBLY EFFECTIVE TEACHING TACTIC #3: HARNESS THE POWER OF FOCUS ANCHORS.

The purpose of using focus anchors is to help you maintain control of the mat in a positive and non-threatening way. Young students, especially, can easily become distracted; and when one student gets distracted, the rest of the students follow suit. In order to bring your class back to task without appearing frustrated or angry, use focus anchors.

RULE OF 3

1.  Keep the anchor strong.

2.  Vary the anchor.

3.  Use focus anchors frequently during the class.

> *Most kids, even the difficult ones, want to be part of the group and they don't want to stand out. When you use a focus anchor, you can get that challenging student back on task without calling attention to him in particular.*

ALWAYS...

Stay positive. Focus anchors get students back on track in a positive way. Use focus claps and/or ask, "Eyes on who?" and have the students respond with the uniform, pre-arranged answer, "Eyes on you, sir!" This gets their attention without any of the negative feelings that can be caused by yelling, "Pay attention, now!" or something like that.

FOCUS ANCHOR TIPS

Use these focus anchor tips to help you keep your classes running smoothly and make them more enjoyable for your students, too!

**Keep the anchor strong**. Use an upbeat yet forceful tone. Don't mumble!

**Vary the anchor**. Using the same anchor over and over will cause students to tune you out, rather than focus in on you. If you run out of ideas, be sure to ask other instructors and Martial Arts school owners. There's a lot of good material out there!

**Use focus anchors frequently during the class**. When you have focus anchors that are used over and over, you can easily maintain discipline on the mat. They can add spice to a class and help build a sense of team membership between the students. Sometimes with an energetic class, you'll need to use a lot of anchors. And that is perfectly okay.

INCREDIBLY EFFECTIVE TEACHING TACTIC #4: ESTABLISH THE HABIT OF POSITIVE PRE-FRAMING.

What is Positive Pre-framing? Positive Pre-framing is giving someone a viewpoint before he has a chance to create one of his own. How does Positive Pre-framing improve Martial Arts instruction? Positive Pre-framing can influence your students to be open and enthusiastic about learning material that is often challenging or maybe even scary.

RULE OF 3

1. Positive pre-frame at beginning of class.

2. Positive pre-frame everything taught.

3. At close of class, positive pre-frame the next class.

*Whether you know it or not, we all unconsciously pre-frame everything we teach. So consciously pre-framing what you do will help you be the best teacher possible. If in doubt, pre-frame EVERYTHING!!!!!!*

ALWAYS...

Take the time to develop and use motivational or positive pre-framing in your classes. If you do this, you will see more enjoyment, involvement, enthusiasm and better retention!

Positive pre-framing is a technique used to get someone to see a situation from a specific viewpoint before they have formed their own viewpoint. The easiest pre-frame is to imply or tell someone what an experience is going to be like and how they are going to react to it. This technique is very powerful and instrumental in influencing people. The secondary benefit of pre-framing is that it causes one to think through what they are going to teach, how they are going to present it, and how the students are going to react to it.

## THE IMPACT OF NEGATIVE AND POSITIVE PRE-FRAMING

Positive pre-framing can make a class. Negative pre-framing can break one! The words you use, the tone of your voice and your physical stance all affect your pre-frame message. Here are two different examples of pre-framing a move—one negative, one positive:

| Negative Pre-frame | Positive Pre-frame |
| --- | --- |
| "You guys are going to have a hard time with this move. It's hard to do and frustrating to teach." | "I'm going to challenge your skill with this next move. You are going to love it and become better because of it." |

While both statements are correct, it should be obvious which one will have a more positive effect on both the students and the instructor.

EXAMPLES OF MOTIVATIONAL OR POSITIVE PRE-FRAMING

At the beginning of class: I have an exciting class planned for you today.

When doing push-ups: All right! We GET to (not have to) do push-ups. You guys are going to get stronger if you do them correctly.

In teaching a new self-defense technique: You are going to love this next move. It develops your ability to…

INCREDIBLY EFFECTIVE TEACHING TACTIC #5: HABITUATE THE 3X3 RULE.

The 3x3 Rule is one of the most important teaching tips to remember because it creates a rapport with your students that will generate loyalty and the desire to continue training with you for years to come.

RULE OF 3

1. Eye contact (3 times during class)

2. Appropriate Body Contact (3 times during class)

3. Use of Name (3 times during class)

> *They will feel that personal connection that lets them know they're not just another body on the mat. Remember, a person's name is his or her favorite word, so use your students' names often to develop lasting relationships that lead to better retention for your school.*

ALWAYS...

To maximize the effectiveness of The 3x3 Rule, try to link all three of them together whenever possible. For example, say their name, look them in the eye, and high five them at the same time.

FOR BETTER STUDENT RETENTION

**Student's Name**. Use each student's name at least three times every day. This can be done before, during and after class.

**Appropriate Physical Contact**. Make appropriate physical contact three times each class. High fives, pats on the shoulder and handshakes are some of the ways to connect with your students each day.

**Eye Contact**. Make eye contact three times. Look your students in the eye when you tell them they're awesome or that you're glad to see them. Your message will be much more powerful and sincere. When you use the 3x3 Rule, it lets your students know that you know they are there training with you.

INCREDIBLY EFFECTIVE TEACHING TACTIC #6: PRAISE PUBLICLY. REPRIMAND PRIVATELY.

Have you ever had the experience of having someone scold you in front of your friends or peers? If you have, you know how horrible that can make you feel, and you can recall that you'd do just about anything to avoid having it happen again.

Make sure you never put your students into that position by remembering the following guidelines for praising or correcting them:

RULE OF 3

1. Reprimand in private.

2. Praise publicly.

3. Never pass up a chance to praise someone publicly.

*Public reprimands are humiliating.*

*Avoid them at all costs.*

ALWAYS...

The easiest way to increase your students' self-esteem is to publicly praise them. If someone does an awesome job, be sure to let everyone know! It will make them feel good and may motivate others to follow her example.

*By employing Public Praise and Private Reprimand, you can*

*build morale (great for students)*

*and retention (great for you)!*

## THE NEGATIVE EFFECTS OF REPRIMANDING PUBLICLY

The easiest way to decrease a student's self esteem is to publicly reprimand him. If you humiliate a student in front of others, he will be less likely to want to come back to class. Corrections to misbehavior, and sometimes even technique, should be done separately from other students, and should be positive and motivating.

Of course, if you're teaching a challenging technique that the whole class needs to work on, you don't need to take each student aside separately. The point is to not single out a particular student and embarrass him or her in front of others.

INCREDIBLY EFFECTIVE TEACHING TACTIC #7: UTILIZE THE 3 D'S —
DEMONSTRATE, DETAIL, DRILL.

Consistent use of The 3 D's will provide your students with a consistently productive experience across the board.

RULE OF 3

1. Demonstrate

2. Detail

3. Drill

> *By implementing the 3 D's in your school, you can increase your students' understanding and skills so that they can have a rewarding learning experience.*

ALWAYS...

Apply The 3 D's to every aspect of your teaching. This will help you be more consistent as a teacher. And your students will know what to expect and actually look forward to learning new moves within the structure of demonstrate, detail, and drill.

THE 3DS—DEMONSTRATE, DETAIL, DRILL

**Demonstrate.** When first introducing a move, it's best to show how it's really supposed to be done. You want your students to say, "Wow! That is so cool! I can't wait to learn that!" By deonstrating the move at the highest level, you motivate your students to want to learn it.

**Detail**. Next, you need to slow down and show the technique in detail. For self-defense moves, you will break it down strike-by-strike, emphasizing body mechanics and targeting. For katas, you will probably only work on one or two moves in detail each class, until you complete the form.

**Drill**. Then, of course, drill, drill, drill. This is where your ability to disguise repetition comes in handy. Make sure that your students have plenty of time to repeat the moves so that they become proficient before you move on to something new.

INCREDIBLY EFFECTIVE TEACHING TACTIC #8: PRACTICE PRAISE-CORRECT-PRAISE.

It is NEVER beneficial to be critical unconstructively. For example, "Your stances are terrible," "Your kicks are sloppy," or "You're always late." This only creates resentment and causes your students to concentrate on their weaknesses rather than on their strengths. It is always much better to be constructively helpful.

RULE OF 3

1. Find something to praise.

2. Correct the problem.

3. Praise the correction.

*Implementing Praise-Correct-Praise helps you correct students in a positive manner. Praise-Correct-Praise feeds their enthusiasm to 'get it right' and learn new moves.*

ALWAYS...

When correcting students, always praise them first. This puts them at ease and allows them to feel better about themselves. Secondly, correct what is being done incorrectly. Finally, praise them after they have made the appropriate adjustments. Always make sure that your praises are specific and not general.

AN EXAMPLE OF PRAISE-CORRECT-PRAISE

If a student is doing a sloppy front kick, you could say, "I like how you keep your guard up. Next time, make sure you lift your knee up high and recoil more." Then with the next kick, you could say, "Good! Your knee was much higher that time."

PRAISE-CORRECT-PRAISE ROLE-PLAYING EXERCISE

Everyone will have a great time with this exercise. Divide your class into teams of three or four. Have them role-play using Praise-Correct-Praise, with one person being the instructor and the others being the students. Make sure each student gets a chance to be the instructor. To make it a little challenging, have one of the students be the designated 'hyper child from your worst nightmare.' Bring everyone back together as a team and summarize the concept of Praise-Correct-Praise.

## INCREDIBLY EFFECTIVE TEACHING TACTIC #9: USE INFLUENCE, NOT AUTHORITY.

The Latin root of the word educate is educo, or to bring out. Excellent teachers bring out the best in their students. But to do this, it's important to use influence, rather than authority. Using authority commands and controls from the outside in, but doesn't bring out the best in anybody from the inside out.

RULE OF 3

1. Influence motivates internally.

2. Authority motivates externally.

3. Always use influence first.

   *Influence is the capacity to cause an effect in intangible ways, whereas authority is the power to command thought or behavior. If someone wanted you to do something, how would you prefer to be guided? With authority or by influence?*

ALWAYS...

If you're like most people, you prefer to be guided and taught as opposed to being told exactly what to do. The same is true of your students. You have the potential to affect great good in the lives of your students and help them rise to the occasion, if you use your influence rather than authority.

## THE DIFFERENCE BETWEEN USING INFLUENCE AND USING AUTHORITY

**Using influence**. When you use influence, you are teaching behaviors that students adopt because they want to. If your way of life and your abilities are appealing, that will cause others to want to emulate you. This is one of the most powerful aspects of teaching Martial Arts.

When you influence your students to follow your example, you are also developing powers of self-discipline that they can then take off the mat and into their lives outside of the Martial Arts school.

**Using authority**. When you use authority, you're using force. Authority has its place, but never on the Martial Arts floor... not if you want your students to continue coming to class, that is.

*Remember to practice using influence instead of authority every day you're on the mat in order to increase student loyalty and retention.*

## PUSHING VS. LEADING

If you push someone, their natural reaction is to push back, to fight you. On the other hand, if you gently take them by the hand and guide them, they will gladly go your way.

## INCREDIBLY EFFECTIVE TEACHING TACTIC #10: ALWAYS FOLLOW THE SMILING-SWEATING-LEARNING RULE (SSL).

Smiling, Sweating and Learning (SSL) should be your goal for every class. You want everyone Smiling, Sweating and Learning! If you consistently reach this goal, you can bet on high retention numbers at your school.

## RULE OF 3

1. Keep your students smiling.

2. Keep them sweating.

3. Keep them learning.

   *Students usually start training in Martial Arts for a few basic reasons: self-defense, fitness, discipline — but they stay for entirely different reasons. They stay because training is fun and enjoyable to them, while providing the benefits of health, fitness and personal safety.*

ALWAYS...

Run your classes according to the SSL Rule. Keeping your students Smiling, Sweating and Learning results in high student retention.

## SMILING, SWEATING AND LEARNING (THE SSL RULE)

**Smiling**. Students don't need to have a smile on their faces to be enjoying themselves. Often, the smile is on the inside when a student is performing a challenging kata with full intensity or during dynamic bag-work.

**Sweating**. You want your students to experience a minimum of 20-minutes of elevated breathing and heart rate during every class. Not everyone will have sweat dripping off of them, because everyone is not at the same fitness level. You just want to make sure there's a good workout in every class.

**Learning**. Students should leave each class with something new. There's so much out there to learn and to teach. Be sure that you are continuing your training so you can share that knowledge with your students. If you repeat the same material over and over, students will become bored.

## INCREDIBLY EFFECTIVE TEACHING TACTIC #11: PRACTICE THE ART OF DISGUISING REPETITION.

Disguising repetition is a very important tool to use to increase attention in class and to eliminate the potential for boredom. We all know that practice doesn't make perfect. Rather, perfect practice makes perfect!

RULE OF 3

1. Change attribute emphasis.

2. Change atmosphere (different environment, different instructor).

3. Change area of focus through non-stop instructor feedback (a lot like the conductor concept of giving nonstop feedback and visual queues to your students as a conductor would give to his orchestra).

*DISGUISE REPETITION.*
*diSGUisE rEPItiON.*
*disguise REPETITION.*

ALWAYS...

Practicing the same thing in the same way over and over is pretty dull, so we must disguise repetition in order to help our students focus on one technique for a longer period of time.

CAMOUFLAGING REITERATION (REPETITION)

**Prepare**. Take the time to prepare your class agenda.

**Explore**. Explore the different aspects of the move: form, accuracy, distancing, speed, timing and power—and how you can develop drills focusing on its different features. Choose a few drills for your current week's classes and others for the following weeks.

**Decide**. Decide if you will have your students practice the move in the air or using equipment such as bags or Wavemasters, or both!

**Mix it up**. By changing up the drills, the students' minds stay engaged even though they are doing the same move.

*Having a planned variety of drills makes class more enjoyable for the students — and you, too!*

INCREDIBLY EFFECTIVE TEACHING TACTIC #12: PRACTICE ZERO DOWNTIME.

It's very important to make sure that there is continuous activity during classes so the students don't become bored or distracted. Strive for Zero Downtime.

RULE OF 3

1.  Plan your class.

2.  Be one step ahead of your class.

3.  Have clear communication between team members.

*It's not how many hours you put in; it's how much you put into the hour. This saying can be applied to our teaching time as well as to our personal time.*

ALWAYS...

Be prepared. The more you practice Zero Downtime, the easier it will become and the more productive and energetic your classes will be.

## AVOID DOWNTIME ON THE MAT

**Plan**. Always plan your class. Know what you're going to do for each segment of the class before you step on the mat. Each segment should flow into the next.

**Stay one step ahead**. Stay one step ahead of the class while you're teaching. While students are practicing a particular technique, go over the next move in your head or let a student know you're going to demo the move with her. When it's time to move on, you're ready!

**Communicate clearly**. If you're team teaching, communicate clearly with the other team members so that you are on the same page regarding the length of your segments, who will be teaching which techniques, and what the overall plan is for the class.

## MAKING ADJUSTMENTS

Following these rules will help you attain Zero Downtime, but sometimes you might have to make adjustments due to circumstances beyond your control. Make sure that if you do have to make changes to your plan, you do it offline. For example, give your students a quick drill to do while you take a moment to reformulate your plan.

INCREDIBLY EFFECTIVE TEACHING TACTIC #13: RISE TO THE OCCASION WHEN WORKING WITH CHALLENGING STUDENTS.

There's no getting around it. Some students are just easier to like and work with than others. It is natural and OK to have favorites. But it is not OK to show it. Not only are there tools that can help you rise to the challenge of training a difficult student, you have the potential of helping that student and transforming a life.

RULE OF 3

1. Build rapport.

2. Give them clear expectations and feedback.

3. Catch them doing something right.

   *Have patience and work positively with each challenging child every time you get a chance and you will be rewarded with some extraordinary black belts in the future.*

ALWAYS...

Apply these rules with all your students without fail. Be persistent. Your efforts will pay off eventually!

RISE TO THE CHALLENGE

**Build rapport.** Make sure to build rapport with your challenging students. If your challenging student is a child, they probably spend a lot of time being scolded, reprimanded and controlled by force or punishment. You want to be the teacher and role model who is a friend, who guides by example, and who is constantly looking for—and finding—the good instead of the bad.

**Give clear expectations and feedback.** Always remember to give clear expectations and feedback. If you have built good rapport, your students will want to please you in order to receive more positive feedback. Make sure that your students know exactly what you want and then enthusiastically let them know when they have met that goal.

**Catch them doing something right.** Finally, catch them doing something right. We all know how good it feels to be recognized for our accomplishments, especially if we're working hard to earn that recognition. Make sure you acknowledge good behavior when you see it, so they will associate the action with the satisfaction of receiving your praise and recognition.

INCREDIBLY EFFECTIVE TEACHING TACTIC #14: MAKE EVERY HUDDLE DISCUSSION A MASTERPIECE.

The Huddle Discussion (also known as a Mat Chat) is an extremely important part of each class. It is our opportunity to share with our students vital messages that can help shape their lives both in and out of the Martial Arts school.

RULE OF 3

1.  Be animated so you hold your students' interest.

2.  Encourage participation.

3.  Be brief and thorough—longer isn't better.

> *Huddle Discussions give you the opportunity to share vital messages that can help shape your students' lives both as Martial Artists and in their personal lives.*

ALWAYS...

Huddle Discussions should be official messages established by your school. On rare occasions, an informal, unplanned Huddle Discussion can be incredibly effective, but it should rarely replace the scripted messages predetermined by your school.

ELEMENTS OF A POWERFUL HUDDLE DISCUSSION

**Be animated and enthusiastic**. Be as animated and enthusiastic as possible. Let your students know that you are interested in the subject you are talking about. If you're interested, your students will be interested. Keep in mind that your level of animation should be in line with the age of the students in your class.

**Ask a lot of questions and role-play**. Remember to ask a lot of questions and do a lot of role-playing. This keeps everyone involved. Huddle discussions should be participatory in nature, never just a lecture.

Keep it brief. Don't spend too much time with a Huddle Discussion. A good Huddle Discussion should take 3 minutes or less. For maximum effectiveness, finish the discussion before anyone's interest wanes.

INCREDIBLY EFFECTIVE TEACHING TACTIC #15: ALWAYS STRESS SAFETY FIRST.

Of course, there are natural risks involved in Martial Arts training and injuries do occur. Fear of being injured and actually incurring injuries are the most common reasons students quit. Knowing and following the proper procedures can minimize the students' fear of being injured, as well as the occurrence of injuries.

RULE OF 3

1. Mindfully pair off partners.

2. Maintain the mat and training equipment.

3. Teach age and skill appropriate material.

*As a Samurai and Martial Arts instructor, your job is to protect your students as much as possible by greatly reducing the risk of injury. And you do that by following the Safety First rule without exception.*

ALWAYS...

- Minimize risk by adhering to the following guidelines:

- Make sure you have students warm up properly.

- Make sure your students are using proper stretching techniques.

- Pair students properly, taking into consideration their size, age, weight, skill, attitude, etc.

- Have realistic expectations and do not ask beginners to do advanced techniques.

- Be aware of your students' limitations, such as their general health, prior injuries, lack of flexibility, fitness level, etc.

- Be aware of space constraints.

- Using safe training aids whenever possible.

IF AN INJURY OCCURS

If an injury does occur, follow these simple guidelines:

- Even for minor bumps and bruises, the parents should be notified. Ice is generally a safe treatment for these types of injuries.

- Have a set policy so your staff knows at what point they should call 9-1-1.

- It's important to keep the class going, if at all possible, while the injured person is being attended to.

- Remind your class of the importance of being calm and that their emotions will influence the injured person's state of mind.

- Make sure that you know how to fill out an accident report.

## INCREDIBLY EFFECTIVE TEACHING TACTIC #16: NEVER COMPROMISE THE INSTRUCTOR/STUDENT RELATIONSHIP.

The bond between Martial Arts instructors and their students can become very powerful. We are teaching life-transforming concepts in addition to the physical arts. Just like when you fell in love with your teacher back in school, your students can develop intense feelings towards you. It is imperative that you understand this and NEVER take advantage of your role as their instructor.

### RULE OF 3

1. Be friendly, but not a friend.

2. Be personable, but not personal.

3. NEVER use your influence on students for selfish gain.

*More casual, friendly relations have their dangers, too, as you can be placed in the uncomfortable position of being taken advantage of by someone you thought of as a friend.*

ALWAYS...

Remember that the instructor/student relationship is all about mutual respect. Be sure to exemplify the concepts you teach by maintaining the proper demeanor with your students.

BE COMPLETELY PROFESSIONAL

In order to be completely professional in your instructor/student relationships, never compromise the instructor/student relationship. This might take great self-control and discipline sometimes, especially in the case of mutual attraction with one of your students or the enthusiastic insistence of a student or parent that you become part of their lives on a personal level. While there are numerous scenarios that could occur, you'll be safe if you follow these simple guidelines.

**Be friendly, but not a friend**. Developing a strong friendship with a student can compromise your professional relationship.

**Be personable, but not personal**. Small talk is fine, but steer clear of talking about the details of your personal life.

**Never use your influence for selfish gains**. It's inappropriate to misuse your influence as an instructor to get a date or purchase something for a discount.

## 16 INCREDIBLY EFFECTIVE TOOLS, TECHNIQUES AND TIPS CHECKLIST

✓ I was friendly on purpose. I warmly welcomed my students and showed a keen interest in them.

✓ I practiced my transformational communication skills. I was aware of my tonality, physiology and physiognomy and the impact they had.

✓ I harnessed the power of focus anchors to maintain harmony on the mat and keep my classes moving forward.

✓ I positively pre-framed each new move and was able to catch myself before I spoke negatively about the difficulty of a move.

✓ I habituated The 3x3 Rule. I made sure that I made eye contact with, used appropriate physical contact, and said the name of each student at least 3 times during classes today.

✓ I protected the honor and dignity of my students. I praised individual students publicly and was able to reprimand in private.

✓ I used The 3 D's—Demonstrate, Detail, Drill—throughout my classes. I was thrilled with how quickly the students picked up some new and difficult moves.

✓ I found something good about each student to praise, corrected them, and praised their improvement. Praise, Correct, Praise works wonders!

✓ I worked to use influence—to lead by example—rather than use authority. The students really responded positively to this and my classes went much more smoothly.

✓ I kept my students Smiling, Sweating and Learning (SSL) today. Everyone had a great time and felt really good about the class.

✓ I was well prepared and had a blast Disguising Repetition by using different drills and equipment to practice the same move. Each drill for the same skill felt new and exciting. My students were completely engaged.

✓ My teaching teammate and I practiced Zero Downtime and figured out how we could improve our teaching and communication. We covered for one another seamlessly when either of us needed to step off the mat and kept the students working. In fact, they weren't even aware when there were issues that were being addressed.

✓ I rose to the challenge of teaching difficult students. I was extra conscious of the need to build rapport with them, let them know what I expected and how they were doing, and saw and celebrated what they were doing right.

✓ I carefully chose the day's Huddle Discussion for each class and planned the role-play.

✓ I reminded my students that Safety Comes First, that they don't have to compete with anybody else, and to adjust their workouts if they're unable to perform an exercise without the risk of hurting themselves.

✓ I was highly professional at all times with my students personable, but not personal, and I caught myself being tempted to be much more casual with certain people and checked it.

# STUDENT/PARENT COMMUNICATION

CHAPTER 4

*Communication in all its forms is an integral part of a successful Martial Arts school. Many of the challenges facing most schools are a direct result of poor communication in at least one area.*

Generally speaking, good communication is always the responsibility of the communicator, not the person with whom you are communicating. Students want to know how they are doing. Parents want to know how their children are doing. Some important tips to remember:

1.    Know as much about your students as possible: occupation, service clubs, team sports participation, hobbies, etc.

2.    Have structured progress checks to review progress and set new goals.

3.    Give out report cards and feedback forms.

4.    Give frequent, impromptu feedback (especially positive) to students and parents.

5.    Give frequent, sincere praise.

6.    Spread the wealth as evenly as possible by talking talking to everyone.

7.    Connect with each and every student during every class. Make sure they know that you know they are there.

8.     Only use humor that builds the student up.

9.     If you are wondering if a certain comment is appropriate, don't make it (in the wondering is the answer).

10.    Do your best to be as enthusiastic as possible.

11.    Show no favorites. It's natural to have favorites, but no one should be able to tell who they are.

12.    NEVER say anything to a child that you wouldn't say if their parents were listening.

13.    Generally speaking, adults want specifics on how they can improve. Give it to them.

14.    Never speak down to students, especially adults. In many  cases, they may be both older and have more life experience than you have. Always treat them with respect.

15.    Whenever possible, give positive feedback to parents regarding their child's progress. Nothing makes a parent happier than hearing about how well their child is doing.

*In an effort to minimize potential miscommunication with its students, the easiest thing for a school to do is to over-communicate using a variety of methods—such as announcements, email, texts, handouts, web pages, etc.*

## COMMUNICATION BREAKDOWNS

**Challenge #1**: A high percentage of students quit right after earning their Black Belts. Possible Communication Breakdown: Failure of the instructor to communicate the benefits and fun of training after earning a Black Belt.

**Challenge #2**: Several students show up on a day that the school cancelled classes due to a special event. Possible Communication Breakdown: Current events are not being announced effectively.

**Challenge #3**: Parents are upset because their child isn't ready to promote when he was originally supposed to. Possible Communication Breakdown: Weeks before, the instructor didn't start pre-framing the family on the importance of attendance and/or home practice and how that relates to steady progress.

## HOW TO COMMUNICATE WELL WHEN A CONFLICT ARISES

There is inevitably going to be a difference of opinion or a conflict arising from poor communication on an individual basis. As a modern day Samurai, communicating with honor and respect is paramount and will help everyone find a solution. The following guidelines are useful when communicating with adult students and parents, as well as with fellow instructors and other coworkers.

**Be unemotional**. Logic and emotion are like oil and water; they don't mix. If you speak calmly and logically, chances are the other person will respond in turn. Also, have a solution in mind. Whenever possible, go into the discussion already having a potential solution to which the other person will be receptive. But be flexible and also willing to adjust.

Rather than be on the defensive, seek first to understand and then to be understood. In other words, try to see the other person's viewpoint before expressing your own. This is important! People can sense when you are trying to understand how they feel and are therefore much more receptive to understanding your views, opinions and ideas. Secondly, you just might see the validity of what they are saying.

What else? **Don't be a nitpicker**. Avoid bringing up unrelated stuff that is not pertinent to the conversation. Nitpicking tends to make people defensive and never helps to resolve anything. Resist the temptation to argue. If you aren't sure what to say or how to respond, say nothing. Be sensitive to others' needs and feelings. To a hammer, everything is a nail. Each situation is different, each person is different, and so each situation and person should be treated accordingly.

**Keep things impersonal**. Discuss the actions with which you are concerned but do not make it about the person, which feels offensive and accusatory. Use I feel, I felt or I found rather than presenting your viewpoint as hard facts. Reaffirm and restate their value and strengths. People are much more receptive to input when they know that you appreciate their other qualities. In other words, remember to Praise-Correct-Praise. Lastly, agree to disagree. It's okay to hold different viewpoints, as long as there is mutual respect and a way to work around it.

## EMPOWERING QUESTIONS TO ASK PARENTS

These questions are designed to help shy instructors get comfortable speaking with parents.

1. Do you want to hear how well your child did in class today?

2. What are some of the benefits that your child has received from training at our school so far?

3. What part of class do you feel is the most empowering for your child?

4. Has your child done anything recently that you are proud of that you would like me to acknowledge?

5. How else can we assist with your child's growth?

## STUDENT/PARENT COMMUNICATION CHECKLIST

- ✓ I know as much about my students as possible: their occupations, service clubs, team sports participation, hobbies, etc. And I am always seeking to learn more.

- ✓ I have scheduled progress checks to review progress and set new goals.

- ✓ I give out report cards and feedback forms.

- ✓ I give frequent, impromptu feedback (especially positive) to students and parents.

- ✓ I give frequent, sincere praise.

- ✓ I spread the wealth as evenly as possible and talk to everyone.

- ✓ I connect with each and every student during every class and make sure they know that I know they are there and care about them.

- ✓ I only use humor that builds the student up, never sarcasm.

- ✓ When I am tempted to make a comment I am unsure about, I do not make it.

- ✓ I always do my best to be as enthusiastic as possible.

- ✓ I never show favorites.

✓ I never say anything to my students that I wouldn't say to their parents.

✓ I give my adult students specifics on how they can improve.

✓ I never speak down to my students, especially the adults. I respect that they have more life experience than I do and I always treat them with respect.

✓ I look for opportunities to give parents positive feedback regarding their child's progress.

# ETHICAL RECRUITING AND REFERRALS

CHAPTER 5

## PERSUASION POWER

The first step to being able to effectively recruit students for your school is to fine-tune your power of persuasion. Every good teacher has a high level of persuasion power.

## RULE OF 3

1. Likeability

2. Enthusiasm

3. Trustworthiness

*If you practice likeability, enthusiasm and trustworthiness on a regular basis, you can become more persuasive and move your career forward along the path to success!*

### LIKEABILITY, ENTHUSIASM AND TRUSTWORTHINESS

**Likeability**. Remember, people prefer to do business with people they like and enjoy being around. With whom would you rather do business, the grumpy, unsmiling and indifferent worker or the warm and friendly employee? Try to be the instructor you'd like to teach you!

**Enthusiasm**. If you're enthusiastic about the benefits of Martial Arts and teaching it, people will more likely become interested. If your energy exudes confidence in and willingness to support your students, those feelings will rub off on your potential parents and students. Then they'll feel secure and confident enrolling in your school.

**Trustworthiness**. Trust is usually not given easily, especially if a student has had bad experiences in the past. In order to quickly earn the trust of your students and the younger students' parents, be sure to present yourself professionally at all times. Nowadays, this can be a challenging task. You don't want to appear too formal, but you don't want to be overly casual either. Take your cues from your student and always err on the side of being more respectful over more casual.

## EXTERNAL RECRUITING

### EVERYONE YOU MEET IS A POTENTIAL STUDENT

It's very important that you remember that it's a small world while you go about your personal business outside of your Martial Arts school. Everyone you meet— at the grocery store, a restaurant or your own children's school— is a potential customer. You should treat everyone with courtesy and respect always, no matter what the situation is.

**Self-control and good manners**. Treating others with consideration and politeness, especially when it's tough, is the right thing to do. When you find yourself in a difficult or challenging situation, acting with self-control and good manners will diffuse the situation and lead to a positive resolution.

**Walk your talk**. There's a good chance that that person you treated with respect during that difficult scenario will walk into your Martial Arts school someday and recognize you. And you can bet that he or she will remember how you handled yourself and responded to them. They will be more likely to interact with and trust you because they know you walk your talk personally and professionally.

*It's always better to have friends than enemies. As you walk through your daily routines, remember to leave a trail of friends behind you and they may soon become your loyal students, as well.*

## GENERAL RECRUITING OUTLINE

### THE IMPACT STATEMENT

The impact statement is designed to create an impressive, "Wow, I had no idea that Martial Arts did all that. My family and I should enroll right away!" effect anytime someone asks a question about Martial Arts.

### THE SCRIPT

**Instructor**: "Let me tell you, training at [name of your school] can be life transforming. It has been amazing to see the positive impact it has on people."

- For adults inquiring about enrolling, follow with: "There are a lot of reasons why you might choose to study Martial Arts at [name of your school]. You'll learn effective self-defense, have increased energy and fitness, better focus and concentration, stress relief, and probably most importantly, it is a great environment and you'll have a lot of fun!"

- For parents inquiring about enrolling their children, follow with: "There are lots of reasons you might want to get your [child/children] into Martial Arts. [He/She/They] will gain improved concentration, balance and coordination, improved fitness and self-defense skills. [He/She/They] will also see an improvement in other sports, a higher level of respect and self-discipline, academic achievement, and, of course, [he/she/they] will have a lot of fun in the process."

- For both adult students and parents considering enrolling their children: "These are just some of the benefits of Martial Arts training. Are you looking to accomplish something in particular?"

- In response to the prospective student or parent's response to the question above: "That's great! Many of our students train with us for the same reason. In fact, we specialize in [reinforce the values & benefits that the person stated]."

"We start all new students with a tour of our school and a *Free Private Introductory Lesson*. This will give us an opportunity to get to know you and answer any questions you may have. It will also give you a chance to experience some of the basic skills we teach and see how much [you/ child's name] will enjoy training with us. Then we'll explain our schedule and enrollment options after that class."

## INTERNAL RECRUITING

### PARENTS IN THE STANDS

This promotional tip focuses on a great source of new students, the parents of your junior students who spend a couple of hours a week at the karate school watching their children in class.

*Remember, just because they won't enroll today,*
*it doesn't mean they won't tomorrow.*
*Keep your conversations positive and upbeat and*
*you will probably gain a student down the line!*

### GROWING YOUR ADULT ENROLLMENT

A large portion of most schools' adult population is made up of parents of junior students, so be sure to follow the tips below to grow your adult enrollment:

**Develop a rapport with the parents**. Learn their names. Talk with them about their children and their own lives. Having an ongoing dialog allows you to take the next step.

**Start the enrollment conversation with leading questions**. Ask if they're happy with their child's progress and if their child is happy, too. Do they see improvements in behavior and attitude that make them glad they enrolled in the program? This will then naturally flow to the main question, "Are you ready to start training?"

**Be prepared**. Know when the next orientation class will be held and have a gi in their size on hand. Let them know if it's Parents Train For Free Month or if you have an introductory offer they can take advantage of.

**Ask permission**. If someone says they're interested, but now is not a good time, ask for permission to bug them later and then be sure to remember to do so. (You might even schedule it in your calendar.) Two to three months is a good waiting period.

**Be respectful**. If someone says they're not interested, be sure to remember that, too. You don't want to keep bugging someone who will never sign up.

## SIBLING SEARCH

Sibling Search is a method of finding new students to enroll at your campus. First, you need to identify the brothers and sisters of your current students who aren't training, but could be. To do this, go through your student roster to find students who have siblings of the right age to begin training. Then, make note of when they normally attend class so you can be prepared to approach the parent and potential new student.

*Satori Academy has lots of families who train together on a regular basis, so we know that siblings are a great source of new students for your campus.*

When approaching the sibling, make sure you know his name and engage him in a short conversation. Be sure to greet the parent, too. Let them both know you think he's ready. Be prepared and know when the next class is and offer to sign him up, if it's okay with Mom or Dad. If they're not feeling ready, ask when you can check back (within a couple of months would be best).

The better you know your students and their families, the easier this is. Greet parents and siblings of your students on a regular basis and get to know their names. Also, talk to your students about their families to find out if there might be siblings who don't come in to watch classes. Then you can ask the parents if that brother or sister might be interested in training.

ETHICAL RECRUITING AND REFERRALS CHECKLIST

✓ I am likeable.

✓ I am enthusiastic.

✓ I am trustworthy and present myself professionally at all times.

✓ I exhibit self-control and good manners in all walks of life, in and outside of the school.

✓ Whenever a challenging situation arises, I handle it with respect and grace.

✓ I walk my talk.

✓ I continually seek opportunities to recruit students. I have my Impact Statement and my script memorized and well rehearsed, so that I'm ready when an opportunity arises.

✓ I learn about the parents in the stand and engage them in friendly dialogue in order to develop a rapport with them. And I seek opportunities to encourage these parents to train.

✓ I've gone through my student roster and know which of my students have siblings who are the right age to train. This way, I'm ready to approach the siblings and their parents to introduce the idea of training.

✓ I know my students' siblings by name and I talk with the parents to ask if that brother or sister might be interested in training.

# STRATEGIES FOR ENHANCED RETENTION

CHALLENGE

VISION

GOALS

SAFETY

SOCIALIZATION

ACCOUNTABILITY

REFLECTION

PUNCTUALITY

APPRECIATION

PROFESSIONALISM

EXCELLENCE

BELIEF

CHAPTER 6

Pretty much everything that we have talked about so far affects retention. The key to great retention is to stack the odds of success in your favor by doing as many right things as possible to keep students.

## STACK THE ODDS OF SUCCESS IN YOUR FAVOR

- Teach great classes. You are only as good as your last class.

- Teach age-appropriate curriculum.

- Teach skill-appropriate curriculum.

- Teach your students the things they enrolled to learn.

- Get the whole family training.

- Keep your students challenged.

- Help your students to set long term goals.

- Keep your students' vision strong.

- Stress safety first.

- Be happy to see your students.

- Encourage socialization.

- Hold your students accountable.

- Know your students' families.

- Get your students involved.

- Encourage reflection.

- Over-communicate.

- Be flexible.

- Be punctual.

- Impeccably maintain your professional appearan; neat and new uniform, good hygienem, and no negatives (wild hair, earrings, tacky slogans on t-shirts, etc).

- Don't take your students for granted.

- Lead by example.

- Be a person your students want to follow.

MAKE THE IMPORTANT SHIFT FROM THE OLD PARADIGM TO THE NEW.

EXAMPLE OF THE OLD PARADIGM

I assume that since Bobby enrolled he will be successful in his training and someday be a black belt.

EXAMPLE OF THE NEW PARADIGM

I assume that Bobby is going to drop out fairly quickly unless we intervene with superior student service.

*Be magnificently obsessed with your students' progress! If you are merely interested your students will just be indifferent. If you are enthusiastic, your students will become interested. If you are motivated, your students will become enthusiastic. If you are inspired, your students will become motivated. And finally, if you are obsessed, your students will become inspired.*

4 CORE BELIEFS THAT UNDERLIE ALL COMMUNICATION.

Beliefs are powerful personal convictions that support your behaviors and attitudes when dealing with other people. In the business of being a Martial Arts school owner or instructor, our beliefs should be apparent whenever we are dealing with our students or potential students. There are four core beliefs that can help your school grow if you incorporate them into your personal interactions with others:

CORE BELIEF #1: THEY ARE INTERESTED.

Whenever you're meeting someone for the first time, or are in a situation where the subject of Martial Arts comes up, believe that the person you are talking to is very interested in what you have to say. Your enthusiasm will potentially lead them to want to learn more.

CORE BELIEF #2: THEY ARE GOING TO ENROLL.

It takes a lot of effort to come in to the campus. The prospective student has probably thought about coming in for a long time and now he or she is taking the next step. If you believe they are going to enroll, your positive feelings will encourage them to sign up for lessons.

CORE BELIEF #3: THEY ARE GOING TO EARN THEIR BLACK BELT.

We've all had that student who started out timid and uncoordinated, who eventually turned into an excellent Martial Artist. If you truly believe that everyone who enrolls in your school has that potential, then you will influence your students to move beyond perceived limitations and attain amazing results.

CORE BELIEF #4: THEY ARE GOING TO TRAIN WITH ME FOR 10 YEARS.

If you've been teaching for a long time, you may have students who have been with you for 10 years or more. You need to believe that if you do everything right; all of your students have the potential of becoming lifelong Martial Artists. Believe that if you never take your students for granted and give them the best experience possible every class, you will earn their respect and long-term commitment.

## RETENTION STRATEGIES CHECKLIST

✓ I teach great classes consistently.

✓ I teach age-appropriate curriculum.

✓ I teach skill-appropriate curriculum.

✓ I teach my students the things they enrolled to learn.

✓ I get the whole family training.

✓ I keep my students challenged.

✓ I help my students set long term goals.

✓ I keep my students' vision strong.

✓ I stress safety first.

✓ I'm happy to see my students.

✓ I encourage socialization.

✓ I hold my students accountable.

✓ I know my students' families.

✓ I get my students involved.

✓ I encourage reflection.

✓ I over-communicate.

✓ I'm flexible.

✓ I am punctual.

✓ I maintain your professional appearance impeccably.

✓ I do not take my students for granted.

✓ I lead by example.

✓ I am a person your students want to follow.

✓ I am magnificently obsessed with my students' progress.

✓ I sincerely believe that the people with whom I share the benefits of Martial Arts are interested in what I have to say.

✓ I expect that the prospective student is going to enroll.

✓ I believe that every student who enrolls has the potential to earn their Black Belt.

✓ I believe that, by always deeply appreciating my students and teaching the best classes possible, my students have the potential to become lifelong Martial Artists and will train with me for 10 years or more.

# THE ANATOMY OF THE CLASSROOM

PREPAREDNESS

ENERGY

ENJOYMENT

VARIETY

STRUCTURE

PRECISION

COMPLETENESS

FUN

STRATEGY

CHAPTER 7

Today's Martial Arts classroom needs to be highly advanced. Long gone are the days of making it up as you go. It is extremely important for instructors to have the skills necessary to break up a class for maximum floor efficiency. They also need to know how to teach the curriculum for maximum overall effectiveness.

## VARIABLES TO CONSIDER

There are several variables to take into consideration when dividing up a class:

- Number of students in the class

- Number and experience of assistants

- Topic being covered

- Age of the students

- Skill level

## FOUR RECOMMENDED CLASS FORMATS

Generally speaking, there are four class formats that we recommend:

1. One Group

2. The Switch Method

3. Circuit Training

4. The 2-Instructor Split

## CLASS FORMAT #1: ONE GROUP

Keep everyone together in one group for the duration of the class. This can be used when the class is small or other experienced instructors are unavailable. If it is necessary to use this format, make sure to change things up, i.e., change directions, partners, drills, etc. This speeds up the pace of the class dramatically, therefore making it more enjoyable for all.

## CLASS FORMAT #2: THE SWITCH METHOD

The Switch Method is a great class format (if run correctly) for a fast-paced, high-energy class. It calls for a minimum of three instructors and works great for a large class. With the Switch Method, the head instructor breaks the class into two primary groups: Group A & Group B. The head instructor keeps Group A and splits Group B into sub-groups led by the other instructors. After 15 minutes, Group A is split into 2 sub-groups to work with the other instructors. Both of Group B's sub-groups then rejoin and work with the head instructor until 5 minutes prior to closing, when all groups are rejoined.

## CLASS FORMAT #3: CIRCUIT TRAINING

The Circuit Training method is a popular class format needing three or more instructors. After warm-up, the class is broken up by age and ability into three equal (or close to equal) groups. Each group goes with one instructor for a pre-determined time, and then the students rotate until they have been with all three instructors. This method is awesome as long as each instructor stays on time.

## CLASS FORMAT #4: THE TWO-INSTRUCTOR SPLIT

The Two-Instructor Split is when the class is divided into two groups (usually after the warm-up) for either the duration of the class or a part of the class time. Near the end, both groups are brought together for closing.

## 10 POWER POINTS FOR A TOP-NOTCH CLASS

1.    Prep Zone

2.    Class Opening

3.    Student Creed

4.    Warm-Up

5.    Classroom Breakdown

6.    Curriculum

7.    Huddle Discussion #1

8.    Cycle Topic

9.    Huddle Discussion #2

10.   Closing

## POWER POINT #1 FOR A TOP-NOTCH CLASS: THE PREP ZONE

The five minutes prior to the start of class is referred to as the Prep Zone. The Prep Zone is designed to accomplish several things:

- Get students to class on time (students come a little early so they don't miss Prep Zone).

- Keep pre-class distractions to a minimum.

- Increase the appearance of structure and order.

- Prepare kids for putting a great effort into class.

- Socialization between students and staff.

Huddle the class on an unused part of the mat in a tight circle:

- Ask them how their day was, what they did in school, etc.

- Review some school rules, martial arts history or some other interesting tidbit.

- Ask them what it takes to be good at Martial Arts.

- Remind them to be super energized throughout class.

## POWER POINT #2 FOR A TOP-NOTCH CLASS: CLASS OPENING

The objective with the Class Opening is to have your students at Level 10 by the time they line up. You want to create an exciting state.

For the ideal Class Opening, call the students out by name, have them race to their spots and high-five their neighbors, while yelling, "Yes, sir!" or "Yes, Ma'am!" as they run out and line up.

After the students have lined up, sell the class by giving a powerful, energized pre-frame of what is going to happen. Review a focus anchor or two and make sure they are strong. Make sure their bows are in tight. Remember, structure creates an atmosphere where self-discipline can develop.

## POWER POINT #3 FOR A TOP-NOTCH CLASS: STUDENT CREED

The Student Creed is one of the pillars of your success. It is one of the key differentiators between Martial Arts and other after-school programs. Make sure you take it seriously. Have your students recite the Student Creed as they stand strong and use strong voices to induce mental and physical focus.

*I intend to develop myself in a positive manner and avoid anything
that would reduce my mental growth or my physical health.*

*I intend to develop self-discipline in order to
bring out the best in myself and others.*

*I intend to use what I learn in class constructively and defensively,
to help myself and others, and never be abusive or offensive.*

Refer to the Creed frequently for motivation and corrections, as there are so many impromptu lessons that can be related to the Student Creed.

## POWER POINT #4 FOR A TOP-NOTCH CLASS: WARM-UP

The Warm-Up should be high energy but familiar. If done in the proper spirit, having a pre-scripted 8- to 10-minute Warm-Up is the best way to start a class. Just as someone can enjoy the same movie or song over and over, students actually enjoy a familiar warm-up routine. It's something they can count on and look forward to...something that they can do well. And it is a great way to start class.

The Warm-Up is designed to acclimate the body for class. First, elevate the core temperature of the body with light cardio, which may include basic calisthenics. Follow up with flexibility training.

## POWER POINT #5 FOR A TOP-NOTCH CLASS: CLASSROOM BREAKDOWN

During the Warm-Up, the instructor should be planning out how he or she is going to break the class up (see the Four Recommended Class Formats).

The transition from Warm-Up to Classroom Breakdown should be quick and seamless, with all assistants standing by ready to take charge of their groups.

## POWER POINT #6 FOR A TOP-NOTCH CLASS: CURRICULUM

At the beginning of every section of class, it is always a good idea to huddle your students together and positively pre-frame the next 15 minutes. Because Curriculum is when new material is generally taught, it is important to stress the 3 D's: Demonstration, Detail, and Drill. Varying your feedback from Group to Individual to Group to Individual (GIGI) will always keep your students' enthusiasm high.

## POWER POINT #7 FOR A TOP-NOTCH CLASS: HUDDLE DISCUSSION 1

Your students have now been in class for 20-25 minutes. They are warmed up, alert, and probably ready for something different. This is a perfect time for your first Huddle Discussion. Remember the three rules of a Huddle Discussion: be animated, encourage participation, and keep it short. (Longer isn't better.) When you have finished, make sure that the transition to the Cycle Topic is quick and seamless.

## POWER POINT #8 FOR A TOP-NOTCH CLASS: CYCLE TOPIC

Generally speaking, the Cycle Topic is the non-curriculum part of class. It might be bag work, sparring drills, self-defense, attribute training, etc. This part of class is more physical, more repetitive, and less structured. The Cycle Topic should be challenging, enjoyable, and give a great workout. Make sure to keep the talking down and the movement up.

Injuries are more likely to occur during this part of class, so always be safety conscious. For example, make certain that there is adequate spacing for the drill, proper partner pairing, well-maintained equipment, etc.

## POWER POINT #9 FOR A TOP-NOTCH CLASS: HUDDLE DISCUSSION 2

The end of the cycle topic is the perfect time for your second Huddle Discussion. Again, remember to be animated, encourage participation, and keep it short. (Longer isn't better.) Whenever possible, position yourself close to parents so they can hear the discussion. When you have finished, make sure that the transition to the Closing is quick and seamless.

POWER POINT #10 FOR A TOP-NOTCH CLASS: CLOSING

Quite possibly, the most important part of class is the last five minutes or Closing. The Closing is your chance to anchor in what your students have learned, make announcements, and positively pre-frame the next class.

End class with a structured, high-energy drill that is fun and that everyone can do well. This is important as it makes students feel good about their training and it looks impressive to the people watching (which is good marketing).

Make sure the Closing bow is crisp and that someone is working crowd control to ensure a smooth transition between classes.

## IMPORTANT STRATEGIES TO USE THROUGHOUT THE CLASS

- Be a Good Finder. Go on a treasure hunt to find the good in each one of your students and let them know what you see.

- Create a private lesson within a group environment by giving students individualized feedback whenever possible.

- Beware of the Masters Stance (standing with your arms crossed looking disengaged). Make sure you look and act like you want to be there.

- Use names whenever possible and don't play favorites. Remember the 3 x 3 Rule.

- Be Animated. Create emotion with motion. Clap, walk, snap your fingers, put your hand by your ear, vary your voice, high five, pat on shoulders, and make faces.

- Make frequent corrections using Praise-Correct-Praise.

- Use Focus Anchors frequently.

- Have students use specific listening positions—sitting, standing, and kneeling. Get your students to focus by having them physically control themselves.

- Make sure to maximize the use of your assistants by:

- Giving them specific assignments and a time limit.

- Hand signals and verbal queues.

- Always show respect to your assistants. Refer to them by last name. Do not overrule them on the floor.

- Constantly be positively pre-framing the future.

- Be ready to accept responsibility and handle parent concerns between classes.

- Police the floor, give extra help when needed, and prepare for the next class.

## ANATOMY OF THE CLASSROOM CHECKLIST

✓ When dividing up a class, I consider all five variables: number of students in the class; number and experience of assistants; topic being covered; age of the students; and skill level.

✓ I stick to one of the Four Recommended Group Formats: One Group; the Switch Method; Circuit Training; or the 2-Instructor Split.

✓ I carefully construct my classes with the 10 Power Points for a Top-Notch Class.

✓ I mindfully design each of the 10 Power Points for a Top-Notch Class for great success.

# WORKING WITH
# YOUNG CHILDREN

FUN

PATIENCE

EDUCATION

PRAISE

ENCOURAGEMENT

RESPECT

DISCIPLINE

CELEBRATION

AWE

CHAPTER 8

Your objectives are the first thing to consider when teaching young kids Martial Arts. If the instructor's objective is to develop a highly skilled 6-year-old Black Belt, good luck. More appropriately, the emphasis for children should be on:

- Teaching them to pay attention so that they can become better learners.

- Developing better coordination so they can become better athletes.

- Teaching them how to be more respectful and courteous.

- Showing them the foundational qualities of cooperation and trust.

- Teaching them basic Martial Arts.

RULE OF 3

1. Make it fun, but understand the difference between having fun and being funny.

2. Keep them busy. Kids have a hard time doing nothing.

3. Be easily in awe.

## GUIDELINES FOR TEACHING YOUNG CHILDREN

Make it fun. This is the most important rule in developing young students. At this age (or for that matter at any age), playing is a big part of life. In order for students to be interested and excel in the classroom, they must have a good time. The class structure of discipline, respect and concentration does not have to be compromised in order to achieve this. Remember, there is a difference between having fun and being funny.

Don't be overly picky about good form. In time you can become more detailed. Initially, however, be happy just having the kids follow along.

Show a lot of examples. Young children learn best by copying other people. If possible, get an older, more skilled student to demonstrate and participate for the duration of the class—and to be a good example for all the little guys and gals to follow!

Change drills often. The average child's attention span is very short. To work with this fact, keep the drills even shorter. Never do any one thing for more than 3 minutes. You can, however, do a lot of repetition if you disguise the repetition.

**Praise effort, encourage participation, and celebrate often.** Initially, it doesn't matter if the students are improving as long as they are trying their best. This is why earnest effort should be praised. Shy students should be encouraged, not forced, to do things. Make it as easy as possible for them to participate and then celebrate their victories, giving lots of high fives and focus claps. Say, "You're awesome," a lot.

**Make a big deal over effort, regardless of where they placed.** So what if someone came in last in the relay race? If you saw them give their very best effort, then go out of your way to let everybody know what a great effort they made.

**Remind students not to compare themselves with others.** When students compare themselves with others, one of two things happens: (1) they get a false sense of superiority or (2) they get a false sense of inferiority. Remind your students that they win whenever they give a good effort.

**Set realistic goals followed by constant feedback.** Students need to have a clear image of where they are going. For this reason, it is important that each student sets specific goals. It is the job of the instructor to help set these goals. Remember that each student has different strengths and weaknesses, which should be taken into account. Feedback is the breakfast of champions. Once goals have been set, give your students constant feedback to help keep them on target.

## WORKING WITH YOUNG CHILDREN CHECKLIST

- ✓ I understand the difference between fun and being funny. And I made class fun.

- ✓ I was excited the kids followed along and I was not overly picky about good form.

- ✓ I had an older, more experienced student demonstrate the moves.

- ✓ I disguised repetition by changing the drills often.

- ✓ I praised my students' effort, encouraged participation, and celebrated their victories.

- ✓ I was in awe of each child and made a big deal over the effort they gave, regardless of how they did.

- ✓ I reminded my students that they win whenever they give it their all and do their best.

- ✓ I helped each student to set goals and I gave them constant feedback.

# TEACHING CHALLENGING CHILDREN

## CHAPTER 9

CLEAR EXPECTATIONS

FEEDBACK

PATIENCE

SELF-CONTROL

POSITIVE REINFORCEMENT

FRIENDSHIP

TRUST

FOLLOW-THROUGH

EMPATHY

GOAL SETTING

UNDERSTANDING

Martial Arts continues to grow in popularity, along with its reputation of enabling people to make positive life changes. With this growing reputation, more and more parents are bringing their challenging children to us in hopes that we can make a difference in their lives.

RULE OF 3

1. Build rapport.

2. Give them clear expectations and feedback.

3. Catch them doing things right.

   *As teachers, our role is to believe that all students (regardless of how they appear) have the potential for greatness. The truth is that way down inside, each child has wonderful, untapped possibilities.*

TEACHING GUIDELINES THAT TRANSFORM CHALLENGING CHILDREN'S LIVES

Although there is no easy way to change or improve behavior overnight, there are some simple teaching guidelines that can help challenging students keep moving in the right direction for lifelong benefits.

**Don't pre-judge**. Teachers have to believe in their students. If you don't believe in your student, your student has very little chance to succeed. All good teachers have seen what many people consider a hopeless student develop into a fine example-setter.

Develop rapport. Respect, trust and, most importantly, friendship are the qualities that need to be developed between instructors and their students. If children respect, trust, and like you, they will be much more receptive to your input.

Keep your temper. Who is a mighty person? Those who have self-control over their emotions and can make friends of their enemies. Teachers should only raise their voices with students if that is what the student needs to hear, not because the teacher has lost control. It is very easy to become angry and take disciplinary action with a disruptive student. Remember, however, that the overuse of punishment strengthens the power of defiance.

Don't threaten unless you plan to follow up. Idle threats quickly become useless when not followed by action. If you say you are going to do something, make sure you do it and make sure that everyone knows that you did. By doing so, the students will be less likely to test you.

Be fair. Make sure the punishment fits the crime. In taking disciplinary action, make sure you're consistent. Being too easy one time and overly hard the next confuses your students.

Catch them doing something right. Most challenging children only receive attention when they are doing something wrong. Sometimes they will act up just to get attention. To break this habit, go out of your way to watch them closely and praise positive behavior, even when it is something minor.

Ask questions. During a disciplinary discussion, ask leading questions and avoid the temptation to lecture. Your influence will be much more powerful if you can get them to tell you why they should or should not do something, rather than you telling them.

Communicate expectations and give feedback. Constantly give these students small, easily achievable goals and keep them apprised of their progress.

Seek first to understand (empathize). Throughout all your interactions, try to see where your students are coming from. You don't have to agree with their viewpoint, just try to understand it.

## TEACHING CHALLENGING CHILDREN CHECKLIST

✓ I believed in my student's ability to succeed.

✓ I worked on developing respect, trust and friendship with my student.

✓ I kept my cool when challenges arose and did not resort to yelling.

✓ I followed through on the disciplinary action and let everyone see that I followed through.

✓ I was consistent and made sure that the punishment fit the crime.

✓ I went out of my way to look for the positive things my challenging student did and praised them.

✓ Rather than lecturing, I asked my students why they should or should not do something.

✓ I gave my challenging students small, easily achievable goals and great feedback on their progress.

✓ I sought first to understand where my students coming from before I shared my viewpoint.

# WISDOM FROM
# THE MAT

CHAPTER 10

## 5 BIG QUESTIONS AND ANSWERS THAT WILL CHANGE EVERYTHING

Several years ago, I came across a series of questions that were originally posed by a man named Ben Zoma, a rabbi in the early part of the 2nd century. I loved the way these questions seemed to naturally tie into the Martial Arts profession. I have used them for years to train my staff.

*The rising tide lifts all boats. If we can all learn to be the very best teachers, the very best motivators, the very best coaches we can possibly be, then our industry is going to continue to rise, grow and prosper.*

**Who is a wise person?** A wise person is one who learns from others. How does this relate to teaching Martial Arts? Have you ever learned something from your youngest child or your most basic beginner? When instructors keep an open mind, they're able to learn important things from others that will make them a better instructor.

**Who is a brave person?** A brave person is one who is smart enough to be afraid, but takes action anyway. What does that mean? As far as teaching Martial Arts goes, it means to be smart enough to be afraid of the responsibility and influence that you have over your students—and then to take that responsibility seriously.

**Who is a rich person?** A rich person is one who appreciates all that they have. How does this relate to teaching Martial Arts? Well, you could be doing a lot of other things, but how fortunate you are to be teaching, developing and working in what? Martial Arts! Don't take it for granted. Every day we should appreciate the fact that we get to teach Martial Arts.

**Who is a mighty person?** A mighty person is one who has self-control and makes friends of his enemies. What does that mean as far as Martial Arts is concerned? Self-control is an important quality that allows Martial Arts instructors to have the discipline to keep themselves in an upbeat, peak state while they are teaching. To make friends of enemies is to win the friendship and trust of your students.

Hopefully you have no actual enemies, but you can apply this concept to your Martial Arts instruction by remembering to treat all students, even the most frustrating and difficult, with the same respect and consideration.  In this way you will earn their friendship and trust.

**Who is an honored person?** An honored person is one who honors others. What does this mean within the context of a Martial Arts class? One who pays respect to students is going to receive respect in return. Respect is the most important quality a Martial Arts instructor can express—to be respectful towards the students and treat them with kindness.

SHOOT FOR ZERO DOWNTIME

One way American Martial Arts has changed over the last twenty years is in the class length. A 2-hour class used to be commonplace. With the exception of special clinics, most successful schools now run 45-minute to 1-hour classes.

When properly executed, there are major advantages to shorter classes. First, long classes have the potential to become boring. Secondly, it is easy for students to over-train and become too fatigued or injured. Thirdly, if students know the class is going to be long they tend to hold back and not put out as much energy or effort. Lastly, it's much easier for people to schedule an hour versus two hours in today's fast-paced society.

Additionally, when teaching 2-hour classes, you have to stretch things out sometimes. With an hour class, you have to work hard to get everything covered. This is the way it should b e because it forces us to plan our classes more thoroughly and then stick with our plan. To maximize your instruction time, shoot for Zero Downtime.

> *Remember, you want your students bowing out of class*
> *thinking, "Is it over already? Wow, that was fast!*
> *I can't wait for the next class!!!"*

Zero Downtime refers to having a well-scripted, educational and entertaining class with no lag time or slow parts.

Ideally, every moment of your class should be scripted—from start to finish—so that there is never a dull moment!

There is probably a veteran teacher reading this right now thinking to himself, "I don't need to script my class. I know what I'm doing." This may well be true. There are many excellent instructors who have a natural sense for how to keep the flow of a class going from start to finish. However, as your classes grow in size and you require several instructors to assist you, then a clear map for Zero Downtime is a must.

*Plan your class thoroughly. Be always one step ahead.*
*Have clear communication between team members.*

SOME ZERO DOWNTIME TIPS

For an engaging, successful class:

**Divide your class time into sections**. Dividing a 1-hour class into four or five sections makes it fast paced and keeps it fresh for everyone, including the instructors.

- Warm-up, stretch, message of the week

- Curriculum

- Skills– topic of the week, such as bag work, sparring, self-defense, etc.

- Drills–fun, high-energy activities, such as group basics, group forms, and games that emphasize Martial Arts attributes like speed, timing, power, focus, etc.

**Divide your class into groups**. When dividing your class into groups, make sure that you plan it out while the students are stretching or busy doing something else. This keeps the class moving versus having them stand around while an instructor decides how to break them up.

**Race against the clock**. For example: After free sparring you might say, "You have 45 seconds to get your gear off and line up. If you have finished sooner, please help someone else with his gear. Ready, set, GO!" This is better than "Try to be the first one done" because that does not promote teamwork.

**Keep your students focused on the present**. Do this by frequently varying the drill a little—change partners or change the direction they are facing. This is often referred to as Disguising Repetition or Camouflaging Reiteration.

**One final note:** Zero Downtime doesn't mean everyone is cheering and clapping from start to finish. Include time for quiet contemplation, a thorough stretch, or a motivational story in your class design and stay on schedule.

## WHO IS A MIGHTY PERSON?

Years back, I was in the middle of taping a series of four ½-hour instructional videos for the Martial Arts Industry Association (MAIA). Each video comprised a combination of Martial Arts drills, skills, teaching tips and a Huddle Discussion for children. I had just finished the third video and was feeling great about them. Experience had shown me that filming can be a fickle experience—I was on fire some days and off on others. This happened to be an on fire day, with only one more video to go. Yes!

I had just finished discussing how a mighty person is one who has control of their emotions and can make friends of their enemies when Sue, my producer, asked to speak with me. When we stepped away from the crew, she quietly told me that we would have to reshoot the first three videos due to technical difficulties.

Instantly, a wave of indignation enveloped me. I thought to myself, "How could this happen! Why didn't she fix the problem after the first episode? Didn't she see how good those takes were?" I was livid and just about to tell Sue what I thought of the situation when it hit me... *who is a mighty person?* If I really believed that a mighty person had control of their emotions, then this was a great chance to practice.

It also hit me that if I tried to reshoot the former three videos in a less than empowered state, they wouldn't turn out very well. Add to this that I'd look pretty silly getting upset after talking about the virtues of self-control.

*Besides, it was an honest mistake and I*
*have certainly made my share of those.*

So I took a deep breath, gathered myself up and calmly told Sue, "No problem." We then shot the four videos in record time and they turned out quite good. What struck me about this incident was that somehow, some way, that day I was able override my initial inclination to become angry. If I did it once, it stands to reason that I can do it again—perhaps even all the time—and so can you! So what do you say? Let's get mighty!

FOCUS FOLLOWS FUN = FUN SQUARED

Have you ever taught a class where everyone seems completely focused, the energy level is high and at the end of the class you know that everyone is leaving stronger, healthier and in a better state of mind than when they arrived? Wouldn't it be great if every class were like this?

*Remember that Focus Follows Fun.*
*Fun is the first step to making every class great.*

When people are bored they tend to lose focus. The trick is to keep them mentally, physically and emotionally stimulated throughout the entire class. This is not a new concept; it's just one that we often forget.

## THE DIFFERENCE BETWEEN HAVING FUN AND BEING FUNNY

As you consider how to energize and focus your class by making it fun, remember that there is a difference between having fun and being funny. Having fun doesn't mean people are laughing and giggling. It doesn't mean your class has to be filled with games. Making your class fun means that you have to structure your class and provide leadership that is enjoyable. This concept is true for students of all ages, not just children. Although the drills might vary with age and skill, the concept remains the same...make each and every class unforgettable! While this sounds great in theory, how can you make it a reality? Let's review some steps that will help you make your classes more enjoyable for all.

*Applying these Five Steps will help ensure that each and every class that you teach is focused and energized!*

## STEP #1: HAVE A PLAN BEFORE CLASS.

It is far too common for an instructor to step out onto the floor, bow in the students and start the warm-up without having a clue as to what he or she is going to teach to the class. With this haphazard approach, the instructor might get lucky and end up teaching a fun, energized and focused class. More often than not, however, the instructor will tend to fall back on old standby drills that the students now know as well as the instructor. The result is most always an average class...at best.

On the other hand, if you plan the class beforehand, your energy and enthusiasm will be very high because you're excited about delivering your well-planned material to your students! We all agree that energy and enthusiasm are infectious. Your focus on your plan, your energy, and enthusiasm are transferred to your students, resulting in a great class where everyone finishes focused and energized. This makes your students want to return for another great experience, thereby reducing attrition.

## STEP #2: DURING CLASS, HAVE THE RIGHT MENTAL ATTITUDE.

While it is important to prepare beforehand, it is also important to have the right mental attitude during class.

*It is absolutely critical to remember that the moment you step onto the mat, your ENTIRE focus and energy need to be directed toward your students. Whatever else is going on in your life, whatever concerns you have, whatever challenges you're overcoming, are irrelevant to that paying student. That student relies on you for energy, focus and enthusiasm. They do not want to hear about your problems.*

Every action every moment must communicate that teaching your class is exactly where you want to be and what you want to be doing. Reciting the instructors creed can help put you in the right mental state: "I will teach this class as if it were the most important class I will ever teach. I am patient and enthusiastic. I will lead by example."

STEP #3: DON'T LET DISTRACTIONS CHANGE YOUR FOCUS.

Distractions occur in every class—an overactive student, a new prospect standing impatiently next to the mat, unhappy parents or some other situation. Whatever the distraction, don't let it reduce the focus, energy and enthusiasm in the classroom. Going back to Step #1 of having a plan to handle distractions before class (having a staff member ready to intercede, for example), can reduce or eliminate the distraction. Keep a clear vision of what you intended for the class. Make whatever adjustments are necessary and keep the class energized and focused.

*Remember that the secret of true concentration*
*lays in the acceptance of endless distractions.*

STEP #4: DEVIATE FROM YOUR PLAN, WHEN NECESSARY.

Every now and then something happens during class that forces you to change the direction of your class. In other words, there are exceptions to the rule specified in Step #3. Use good judgment and determine when it is appropriate to make an exception. It might be a minor emergency that calls one of your assistants off the floor; you may notice some aspect of a student's curriculum that needs extra work; or perhaps your class plan isn't going as you thought it would. In these instances, make exceptions and deviate from your plan while remembering to keep the focus and energy of the students at its peek.

STEP #5: TRACK YOUR PROGRESS.

At the close of each day, make a note of how your classes went. Which drills worked? Which ones didn't? You'll be amazed at how quickly your repertoire of great ideas and drills will increase. The more you track your progress the easier planning for great classes becomes.

There's a great phrase that sums up the attitude you should have about teaching:

*Always be happy, but not satisfied.*

You should be happy with your skill level and happy with your teaching skills. But you should never be fully satisfied with either. There is always room for improvement. Being satisfied implies that you don't care to improve. Happy, but not satisfied refers to the importance of striving each day to become better while enjoying the process.

## THAT'S WHAT I LIKE ABOUT YOU

Martial Arts teachers have enlisted to help their students learn invaluable life skills in addition to those required by Martial Arts. They have the potential to be very influential and effect positive change in their students' lives. This is a noble calling and a grave responsibility.

Therefore, it is very important that we use our influence for the betterment of our students and that our messages are always positive and uplifting. That's What I Like About You is a fun technique that can produce some amazing results. Although it works wonders with our junior students, with a little imagination it can be applied to students of all ages.

"That's What I Like About You" works wonders!

## HOW THAT'S WHAT I LIKE ABOUT YOU WORKS

Imagine that a young student approaches you and says he has a bandage on his finger and doesn't think he can do his push-ups that class. You can respond with, "That's what I like about you, Sam! You can train hard and do push-ups, even when you have a bandage on your finger." It works with practically every excuse—from just being tired to having missed a month of classes, and everything in between. I can't tell you how many times I have successfully used this strategy and it never ceases to amaze me.

*Instead of falling prey to sympathizing or agreeing with students' diminished view of themselves, be sure to build up their confidence by always sharing with them, "That's what I like about you!"*

## WHY THAT'S WHAT I LIKE ABOUT YOU WORKS SO WELL

That's What I Like About You works so well because:

It gives the student a new way to think about how they view themselves. You're literally putting new words into their heads for them to use later.

Rather than being disappointed or criticizing, you are turning the situation into a challenge for the student to perform at a higher level, even though they feel they are facing a difficulty. You're showing them that they can overcome obstacles and still function.

Your students rise to your expectations of them. They start thinking this way even before they come to see you at class: "I'm not really motivated to go to class today, but my instructor expects me there because he knows I train even when I'm tired."

## THE IMPORTANCE OF BEING A TEAM PLAYER

There are few things more important to the long-term success of a Martial Arts school than having a cohesive team. Excellent teamwork makes everything enjoyable, effective and efficient.

## TIPS FOR KEEPING YOUR TEAM IN THE FLOW

**Be loyal to those not present**. No one likes to be talked about behind his back and we should never tolerate people talking badly about others to us. This means that we should speak up and refuse to be a willing listener.

**Do more than your fair share**. We all appreciate working with someone who embodies the spirit of teamwork, seeks ways to help, and pitches in beyond their job description. Develop a reputation for being someone who will do whatever it takes to get the job done.

**Be dependable**. Develop the habit of being where you are supposed to be when you are supposed to be there, ready to do the job.

**Anticipate your partner's next move**. Close teammates rarely need to tell their partner what to do next because their partner has anticipated the need and is already meeting it.

> "See everything. Overlook a lot. Correct a little."
>
> —Pope John XXIII

**Don't vent. Explain**. Nothing is worse for morale than whining or venting to people who aren't in a position to solve the problem. Go to the person who can effect change and then explain your viewpoint in a logical, unemotional manner.

**Be flexible**. Sometimes it is okay to do it someone else's way.

**When giving an assignment, ask. Don't tell**. No one likes to be told what to do, but most are glad to help out when asked.

**When someone assigns you a task, have a great "I'll be glad to attitude."** In other words, be open to input. Humility and generosity will take you far.

**Practice non-judgment**. We are all different, with varied strengths and weaknesses. This is the beauty of teamwork. Each member brings different gifts to the team. Judging our teammates is a poison that undermines both the individual and the team.

**Choose your battles wisely**. If you always have to be right, people will tend to resent you and be resistant to your ideas.

**When at work, put on your game face**. Everyone has personal challenges that they face on a regular basis, but it's important to leave them behind when you're at work.

## HOW TO HANDLE UNHAPPY STUDENTS

Even in the best Martial Arts schools, there are going to be unhappy students from time to time. Sometimes, things just happen and it isn't really anybody's fault. At other times, one party or the other might be clearly in the wrong.

*Regardless of the situation, it is important to understand that winning an argument doesn't keep a customer.*

## NAVIGATING CHALLENGING SITUATIONS

**Be unemotional and non-defensive**. Hear what your student has to say and honestly consider whether or not there is any truth to the complaint. Remember that there are always two sides. If you remain receptive, you will learn things that will help you avoid similar situations in the future.

**Let your student vent**. Sometimes people just want to be heard. Often, they will be satisfied if you listen to them without judgment. Resist the temptation to fire counter-accusations. This can be challenging at times, but it always pays big dividends.

Respond, don't react.

**Ask for a solution**. People will be more receptive to hearing what you have to say if they believe that you are trying to hear their viewpoint. Also, this tends to align both sides and get everyone on the same team.

**Don't take it personally**. Just because an unhappy student is giving you feedback doesn't mean they are criticizing you personally. Remember that feelings aren't right or wrong, they just are.

**Thank them for their concern**. Whatever the outcome, or whether you agree or disagree, sincerely thank your student for his or her interest in your improvement.

**Do what you can to make it right**. The technical name for this is service recovery. When you have made the mistake, doing what you can to make it right goes a long way in turning an unhappy customer into a raving fan.

## NOW IS THE TIME TO BE A MARTIAL ARTS INSTRUCTOR

I conduct a lot of Martial Arts Instructors Boot Camps throughout the United States and beyond. My goal for these camps is to help improve the quality and professionalism of today's Martial Arts teachers. I love visiting the different schools and getting to know their instructors. For the most part, there seems to be a real sense of family among the instructors at these events and a sense of congruency about our professional mission.

## MARTIAL ARTISTS HAVE A UNIQUE OPPORTUNITY TO DO GOOD

Martial Arts instructors are uniquely situated to impact the world in a positive way. I am happy to say that this generation of instructors is light years ahead of where instructors were when I was starting out.

When I began teaching instructors, the concept of presenting yourself in a professional manner and teaching in a structured, empowering way was uncharted territory. Nowadays, it seems to be second nature for most of the instructors with whom I work. Because of this, I can really focus my energy on fine-tuning instructor skills by concentrating on researched, proven techniques and tactics.

## SOME OF THE BENEFITS OF MARTIAL ARTS TRAINING

One of the most important things I focus on is helping instructors to be able to discuss the benefits of Martial Arts training with both current students and potential students.

**Stress**. With everything that is happening in this country and around the world, the stress level of the average person is dramatically higher than in the past. Unmanaged stress can be extremely detrimental to health, relationships and job productivity. Very few things are as effective at reducing stress as Martial Arts.

How many of you have come to the dojo stressed, but left with a completely different mindset? At the end of class, anchor in the good feelings your students have. That conscious memory will make it easier for them to stay in the routine. Remind your students that the next time they consider skipping class, they should remember how good it feels to train.

**Stay-cations**. We know many families who are curbing their travel plans, but who consider their Martial Arts training to be their mini, twice-a-week vacation without ever leaving town.

**Obesity**. Martial Arts is fitness with a purpose. There are few activities that offer the fitness benefits of a good Martial Arts class. Martial Arts training demands a balance between the three components of fitness: strength, flexibility and endurance. A person who trains in Martial Arts will find their weakest areas greatly improved. And because their strength, flexibility and endurance are more balanced, adults and children will be less likely to injure themselves while participating in other athletic activities.

**Athletic Enhancement**. There is a reason why every professional sports team in every major sport supplements their training with Martial Arts. Martial Arts training offers several advantages. It is amazingly effective at enhancing general coordination because it uses every part of the body in a balanced way. Upper body, lower body, right side, left side, forward movement, lateral movement and rotational movement are all included in Martial Arts training.

**Relationships**. The human interaction in Martial Arts classes counterbalances the all-consuming nature of technology. In these days of working at home, 500 cable channels, Twitter and Facebook, many people are starved for quality, live social interaction. At the dojo, students find themselves surrounded by positive, high-quality and encouraging people (instructors and co-students alike) who help to bring out their best and keep them focused on the prize.

## THE WILL AND THE SKILL

I learn so much from visiting different schools and watching instructors teach their craft. The quality of Martial Arts instruction is better than ever.

Today's instructors are far in advance of where my generation was when we were starting out. There are several reasons for this. First, my generation had very few resources for instructor training. Many of us simply thought that being a good Black Belt was pretty much all you needed to be a good teacher. Secondly, we tended to be a bit closed off from other Martial Artists. If they weren't from the same style or association, we usually didn't communicate much. Finally, there wasn't as much competition for students as there is today, which allowed mediocre instructors to stay in business without having to improve. The popularity of Martial Arts has grown so much that the current climate is highly competitive. To stay in business, let alone thrive, instructors must be good.

*To be a successful Martial Arts instructor in a highly competitive environment, you must have the will and the skill.*

## WHAT THE WILL AND THE SKILL MEAN

**The Will**. You have to want to teach. You must enjoy the process. Having the Will means that you look forward to teaching your classes—that you relish the challenge of helping your students to thrive in their Martial Arts quest. Having the Will is the most important quality I look for when I'm hiring. I would much rather employ an instructor with boundless enthusiasm and novice teaching skills than a seasoned veteran who is just trying to get through the week.

**The Skill**. The Skill refers to knowing how to teach. Possessing the necessary Martial Arts skills is important, but being a skilled teacher is vital. Martial Arts and teaching skills are two very different animals. There are many talented Black Belts who have no clue as to how to run a class.

*Once you stop trying to be better, you quit being good. This concept resounds in teaching Martial Arts.*

## SUSTAINING THE WILL AND THE SKILL

It's very easy for most people to fall into a comfort zone. I have been teaching Martial Arts for the better part of forty years and I have had a full-time school since 1978. While I have learned a lot over the years, I know that I have just scratched the surface of possibilities. When I stay mindful of ho impactful Martial Arts can be for people, I am able to keep my will to teach strong. And when I keep an open mind to new and different teaching methodologies, I am able to add new skills to my teaching arsenal.

## KEEP YOUR BLACK BELTS IN THE GAME

Never assume that your Black Belts don't need encouragement to continue their training. I learned this the hard way.

Dan was a second-degree Black Belt and had been training with me for over seven years. He was an all-star kind of guy. He was extremely successful in business, had a great attitude, and was athletic and intelligent. Dan was the ideal student because he inevitably raised everybody's energy level during class. And he was consistent; he never missed a class.

One day he pulled me aside to tell me that his attendance was going to be a bit sporadic over the course of the next month or so due to the opening of a new branch office a city away. I thanked him for the letting me know and told him what I tell everyone who has to deal with a busy schedule: Don't stress over it; just get in when you can and we will make sure to work with you if and when you need the help.

The next time I saw Dan in class was a couple of weeks later. We had started an advance kata just after he left. For the first time ever, Dan was behind the curve. He was doing his best to follow along, but I could tell that he was frustrated. I almost pulled him aside to work with another advanced student but decided against it. After all, this was Dan we're talking about. He doesn't need any extra help. He continued to be sporadic in attendance over the next few weeks and I could sense his frustration growing. Once again, instead of offering him one-on-one help like I would most people, I just let him struggle. Although Dan was not an arrogant guy, part of me felt like this experience was a good way to keep him humble.

I didn't see Dan for a few more weeks and when I did, it was at the end of class and he was in his street clothes. I thought to myself, "That's funny,

Dan must be injured or something." He asked to speak with me privately so we went into my office. He said he wanted me to know how much he appreciated the training he received at our school these past 7-1/2 years and then let me know that he was quitting. I was shell-shocked.

When I called him on it, he simply responded by saying that he was going to continue to be working extra hours and didn't want to be a mediocre student. He said he didn't like the feeling of not knowing what was going on and needing extra help, and it had taken the joy out of his training. I assured him that I would work with him after class or on weekends, whatever it took to keep him training, but it was too late. He'd made up his mind. And so we said our goodbyes. That was the last time I heard from Dan.

*I can't help but believe that if I had taken the time to work with Dan just a little bit extra instead of letting him flounder, he would still be training with us to this day.*

Dan quitting was a great lesson for me. It reminded me that even Black Belts get discouraged and quit, and that I should never take any of my students for granted. If I see a student struggling, regardless of rank, it's my job to help them get back on track. And it's yours as well. The next time you see advanced students who need a bit of help, think of Dan and then do what you can to keep them in the game.

## 10 STUMP SPEECHES THAT EXPLAIN THE BENEFITS OF MARTIAL ARTS TRAINING

Several years ago, I visited my friend Keith Hafner in Ann Arbor, Michigan. Keith runs an amazing Martial Arts school. His ability to articulate the benefits of Martial Arts training to his students stood out. I was so impressed with the way he explained the benefits of training that I wrote a bunch of Stump Speeches (Miagi-isms) so that my staff and I could try to do the same. These Stump Speeches discuss various benefits of Martial Arts training and can be memorized and internalized so that you can easily call on them whenever needed.

### STUMP SPEECH #1: EMPOWERMENT

We often feel powerless. By showing us how to dramatically increase physical power through conditioning and proper body mechanics, Martial Arts empowers us in every aspect of our lives.

### STUMP SPEECH #2: PHYSICAL BALANCE AND SELF-CONTROL

We often feel out of balance. By learning proper stances, efficient movement and striking skills, Martial Arts helps us to know what it feels like to be balanced physically. And physical balance is directly related to emotional control.

*Concentrate on your balance, lose your upset.*
*Concentrate on your upset, lose your balance.*

## STUMP SPEECH #3: FLEXIBILITY AND OPEN-MINDEDNESS

We are often very rigid. We are resistant to new ideas or change. Martial Arts helps us develop more flexibility, and teaches us to loosen up and become more open-minded and receptive to feedback.

## STUMP SPEECH #4: QUICK REACTIONS AND A MORE MANAGEABLE PACE

We often feel like things are coming at us too fast and we can't keep up. By learning how to strike with speed and defend quickly, everything else seems to slow down and be more manageable for us.

## STUMP SPEECH #5: VITAL ENERGY AND MENTAL TOUGHNESS

We often feel tired and sluggish. By developing our physical stamina, Martial Arts not only increases vital energy, but also helps develop mental toughness to get through life's biggest challenges.

## STUMP SPEECH #6: REACHING GOALS AND LIFELONG CONFIDENCE

Many people spend more time planning their vacations than planning their lives. By achieving short- and long-term training goals (like tips and belts and, ultimately, a Black Belt), Martial Arts instills lifelong confidence in one's ability to set and achieve worthy goals in all areas of life.

## TUMP SPEECH #7: SELF-CONTROL AND STAYING CENTERED

We often feel out of control, a slave to our impulses and emotions. By learning how to control our movement and techniques—and focusing our energy and emotions on the task at hand—Martial Arts develops the innate ability to stay centered and focused on the present moment in even the most stressful of times.

## STUMP SPEECH #8: RESPONDING TO DANGEROUS SITUATIONS AND MEETING LIFE'S CHALLENGES

We often feel fearful or uncertain about how to respond to the environment around us. By learning how to discern the difference between unwarranted fear and real danger (and then how to respond in dangerous situations), Martial Arts helps us to develop real confidence in the face of adversity.

## STUMP SPEECH #9: GIVING AND GETTING RESPECT

Many people lack respect for themselves and those around them. Or perhaps they feel that no one respects them. By teaching us to give and receive respect—and developing a new appreciation of our body and our evolving skills, Martial Arts brings out a natural feeling of respect which permeates every aspect of life. And we learn to understand that in order to get respect from others, we have to give it.

STUMP SPEECH #10: DISCIPLINING OUR BODIES OPENS UP LIFE'S POSSIBILITIES

Most of the time we know what we should be doing to improve our lives, but we lack the discipline to do it. By disciplining our body to learn and perform new skills and by sticking to a set practice routine, Martial Arts fosters the self-discipline that makes all other things possible.

*Someone who has self-discipline knows what to do and does it.*

## UNDERSTAND THE VALUE OF POSITIVE RITUALS FOR PROFESSIONAL AND PERSONAL GROWTH

Take care of the days and the years take care of themselves. This concept is so simple, it is often overlooked or dismissed in search of something more advanced or complicated.

Jim Loehr and Tony Schwartz's book, The Power of Full Engagement, explains the importance of developing positive daily rituals...that long-term success can be directly related to the number of positive rituals an individual has developed.

Analyze your day from start to finish. What has become your routine? When do you wake up? What do you eat for breakfast? What books do you read? Do you exercise? Once you've done this for a day (better yet, a week), go back and decide if what you are doing is what is most beneficial to you. If it is, keep going. If not, what can you do differently?

## A NOT-SO-HEALTHY MORNING ROUTINE

Imagine that every morning you wake up late, rush out the door without breakfast, and grab a doughnut on the way to the office while listening to talk radio.

## A HEALTHIER MORNING RITUAL

Now imagine that every morning you wake up early, enjoy a tall glass of water, have a brisk workout, and take time to read some positive literature while enjoying a nutritious breakfast.

## IMPORTANT QUESTIONS

How does the not-so-healthy morning routine compare with the healthier morning ritual over the course of ten years? Physically, how different will you look? Emotionally, how will you feel? Professionally, where will you be? And spiritually, how centered will you be?

## A FULL DAY OF POSITIVE RITUALS

Chances are you can see how different your life would be by just developing a positive morning ritual. Now magnify this concept by imagining a full day ruled by positive rituals. What would such a day look like? Write out your ideal day in detail. When would you exercise? What would you read? What would you eat? With whom would you spend time? Where would you live? How would you treat the people around you? The more detail, the better. When you have finished, read it daily and do your best to make your perfect day become a positive reality.

## COMPETING WITH OTHER SPORTS AND KEEPING YOUR STUDENTS' TRAINING

We've all had our share of students who quit because of the demands of participating in another sport. Most tell us that they will be back after the season, but this is rarely the case. When the season has wrapped, it takes a lot of effort to get back into the routine of Martial Arts. Add to this that the students feel like they have forgotten a lot and their friends are a belt ahead of them. As Martial Arts instructors, we know that it is in the best interest of our students and our schools to keep them training through the season.

### STRATEGIES FOR KEEPING STUDENTS TRAINING WHO ARE INVOLVED WITH OTHER SPORTS

When a student expresses the need to take some time off training due to involvement in another sport, the first thing you need to know is whether or not they are happy with their lessons so far. If they are unhappy, they might be using another sport as an excuse to quit. In this case, all your persuasion skills will be for naught.

If they are happy with your program, then you should be able to keep them training. A simple, "How are you enjoying the program?" is a good place to start. If you get a lukewarm response, probe a little deeper to find out why they are not completely satisfied with your program. At the very least, you will be able to discern if there are steps you can take to tighten up the program so you won't lose more students for the same reason in the future.

If you find that the student loves the program or that the parents see its benefits for their child, then sit down with them, review the schedule for different time options, and let them know that it is okay to miss some classes. Emphasize that by continuing to train, even sporadically, they won't fall behind. Another option is to offer special 15-minute one-on-one classes to keep the student current.

## ROLEPLAYING: CONVERSATION WITH A PARENT

**Parent:** I need to put Johnny's training on hold because soccer just started and we are just too busy.

**Instructor:** I bet you are extremely busy. Do you have a few minutes to talk about it?

**Parent:** Yes.

**Instructor:** Great!! First off, before we go forward, I wanted to know how you have liked the program so far.

**Parent:** It has been great...just what Johnny needed.

**Instructor:** How has Martial Arts benefited Johnny exactly?

**Parent:** Well, there are a lot of things. His behavior has been better. He is much more confident now. And his coordination has really improved.

**Instructor:** Do you think it will help his soccer game?

**Parent:** Oh, yes!

**Instructor:** Can you see how keeping Johnny training until he gets his Black Belt will continue to help him?

**Parent:** Absolutely! Don't worry. We have no intention of having him quit. He will be back right after the season is over. It's just that we have to take a break because we just have too much going on.

**Instructor:** Mrs. Smith, I'm sure that that is true. Just let me share with you a couple of concerns I have and then some probable solutions, okay?

**Parent:** Okay.

**Instructor:** Mrs. Smith, there is a phrase that we use: Sometimes maintaining is gaining. It basically means that if we can find a way to keep Johnny's foot in the door during the soccer season, he will be way ahead of where he would be otherwise. You see, at the end of the season, his friends will be a Belt ahead; he'll feel like he has forgotten everything, and you'll be out of the routine of bringing him. I can't tell you how many times that someone has stopped going for soccer season and then never got started again.

**Parent:** Well, what do you suggest?

**Instructor:** First off, let's take a look at the schedule. Right now Johnny comes on Monday and Wednesday. Did you know we have a Tuesday and Thursday schedule as well?

**Parent:** I'd forgotten. But I just can't get him in twice a week.

**Instructor:** Is there a way you can try to get him here once per week and then, during the season, maybe you can bring him in on a Friday or Saturday a couple of times for some one-on-one training?

**Parent:** Well, I am not sure. We are just so busy.

**Instructor:** How about we just try it out and see how it works? Then in a couple of weeks, we can revisit it to see how it's going.

**Parent:** Okay.

**Instructor:** Great! So what day are you going to try to get Johnny here?

## DRAMATICALLY INCREASE RETENTION WITH A BLACK BELT CLUB

Offering membership in a Black Belt Club (BBC) or a similar designation in your school is a powerful tool that can be used to increase retention dramatically. I'm often asked about how we structure our Black Belt Club. What kind of a discount do members get on retail? Do we have a special class only for them? Do they get to wear a cool uniform? For how long do they enroll? The truth is that our Black Belt Club doesn't have anything to do with wearing a red gi that has a neon BBC patch on it...or enrolling in a 3-½ year program...or having a special members-only training class. There is nothing wrong with any of those things, but the real goal of the BBC is to have the students make a public commitment to getting their Black Belt.

*By focusing on getting a Black Belt commitment from your students, you can build retention and ensure the future of your Martial Arts school.*

## PUBLICLY MADE COMMITMENTS ARE POWERFUL

It is a lot more challenging to go back on a promise that has been made publicly. The instructor's goal is to have their students commit during the BBC meeting and make the promise publicly by wearing a patch or announcing the goal in front of a class. The BBC Commitment that our students sign has nothing to do with money. Rather, it is a simple pledge of commitment.

*The BBC Commitment: I am committed to obtaining the rank of Black Belt and am willing to do what ever it takes to do so. I also understand that my instructor will not let me quit and will be there every step of the way to help me reach my goal.*

## BLACK BELT COMMITMENT DETAILS

When you perform the BBC interview, encourage your students to promise publicly and personally that they will earn their Black Belt. Then, if the students ever waver in their commitment, you can recall that meeting and pull out their written promise to persuade them to keep pushing through a challenging time. Remind them that you don't know of anyone who is sorry they earned their Black Belt, especially those who considered quitting at one time or another.

Remember that in order for this to work most effectively, your school must be running well and be able to meet the needs of your students. Be sure to make an honest assessment of the product you're offering if you hear from multiple students that they're thinking of quitting.

## KEEP BELT PROMOTIONS EXCITING AND FRESH

How many belt promotions have you done at your school? If you've been teaching Martial Arts for a while, you know the belt promotion drill so well you could probably run one in your sleep. And that's the problem. You're so familiar with belt promotions that it's easy to go on autopilot. And when you go on autopilot, the event is lackluster and the students feel that.

## BIG BENEFITS FROM GIVING EVERY BELT PROMOTION YOUR BEST EFFORT

**Parents will be reminded how great your program is.** For some parents, belt promotions are the only time they come into the school. If they see a dazzling belt promotion and if their child shines at the event, they'll leave with a strong feeling that your program is great for their child. If they see a lackluster promotion and if their child does just okay, they may begin to feel that it's time for their child to try something new.

**Children will be reminded how much they love Martial Arts.** The journey to earning a Black Belt takes years and, inevitably, most children will get bored or discouraged along the way. But if the children are well prepared for their promotion and if the promotion event is brilliantly executed, they walk onto the mat with confidence and perform at a very high level. Everyone in the audience is smiling at them. They feel great! And suddenly they remember how much they love Martial Arts! Quitting is the last thing on their mind!

Guests at the event will want to get in on the fun. Here's the scene: You're running your best promotion ever! The kids are sharp. Your staff is at their very best. The event is well paced with just the right mixture of fun, seriousness, showmanship and top-notch demonstrations. Everyone in the audience is impressed. You can be sure that many of those in attendance will be curious to learn more about your programs.

TAKE YOUR BELT PROMOTIONS TO THE NEXT LEVEL

**Get your students to pack the school with their family and friends**. Every promoting student should have at least two people come to the Belt Promotion. The more the better! It's fine if your other students want to come to support the friends they train with, but your goal is to pack your school with people who may like what they see so much that they want to start and/or they can't wait to tell others how great your program could be for their children. You may want to use simple printed invitations.

**Before the event, make sure that you school is ready**. Imagine that the governor of your state is coming... and your mom. Clean everything! If you use chairs, get them in nice neat rows. If you use a sound system, test the levels to be sure they're just right. If you have anything on your counter, be sure it's neat. Neaten every piece of gear. Make your school look as sharp as the day you opened.

**Before the event, make sure that your students are ready**. Be sure they know exactly what they'll be doing at the event. You don't want them to feel tentative and nervous. You want them to feel confident and excited, so that they'll shine. Practice in class before the event and have them arrive early for a dress rehearsal. This particular Prep Zone can play a huge role in the success of your promotion.

**Before the event, make sure that your staff is ready**. Be sure that everyone knows exactly what to do during the promotion. Have a quick huddle before you get going to go over your objectives and expectations.

**Put on a great show!** Every great show has a great structure. Here's an overview of what we do:

- **Opening:** Welcome everyone and fire up the crowd!

- **Demonstration:** If you have a demo team, have them do a brief but dazzling routine. If you don't have a demo team, get some top tier students do the demo.

- **Review the benefits of what your students have learned:** Ask students what they enjoy most about their training and what benefits they're getting from their training. (Important—do a dry run with them before the promotion so you know who gives the best answers.)

- **Curriculum review:** This should be short and sweet. Be sure to make your students look great!

- **The Promotion:** Belt Promotion is a meaningful ritual. Make it a big deal. A little Martial Arts mystique adds a lot. Remind them that A Black Belt is a White Belt who never quit, and while there are sometimes challenges along the way, no one ever regrets earning their Black Belt.

- **Closing and Call to Action:** Thank the students and their guests. Wrap up the event with gentle encouragement for anyone to give your program a try. (If everything went well, at least half the audience should already be thinking about this.) Let the audience know that if anyone would like to learn more about your programs, to please feel free to ask any of your staff.

**After the formal event, circulate in the crowd**. Congratulate students and parents. Smile for pictures! Look for younger siblings who may be ready to start. If anyone looks even slightly interested, ask them if they've ever considered training.

BELT PROMOTION OBJECTIVES

- To bring in a big audience of prospective students (kids, parents and potential adult students).

- To have every student who promotes leave the event more committed than ever to continue their training.

- To have every parent of your younger students leave the event more committed than ever to having their children continue their training.

- To entice everyone in the audience to give your program a try.

## BRING YOUR A-GAME EVERY DAY

*The general manager of Kovar Systems, Mark Seidman, put the following piece together for one of our staff meetings. It is so good that I had to share it with all of my Martial Arts Instructor friends.*

Imagine for a moment that you just found out that Chuck Norris is in your city shooting some scenes for his next movie. And you've just been notified that he would like to visit your school tomorrow to get in a little training after a long day on the set. He knows he can't be anonymous, but he just wants to get in some training with your advanced adult class. After you verify that this is not a hoax, you spring into action:

You call your staff together and let everyone know that they need to bring their A-game. You review your plans for every class to be sure everyone is on the same page and ready.

You make sure that your school looks as sharp as the day you opened it. Your mats are cleaned. Your bathrooms are spotless. Your office is immaculate. Every sign is perfectly straight. Every piece of gear and furniture is exactly where it is supposed to be. You replace any burnt out light bulbs. Maybe even a candle or two to be sure the place even smells perfect.

You walk outside and take a good look at your school from the street to be sure that it looks great when he arrives. You pick up every piece of trash within 10 yards of your door. You make sure that your staff has moved their cars so he can get a good parking space.

You've been told that he might get there early, so you make sure that every class that day runs like clockwork.

To be sure that everything goes perfectly, you make sure to have enough help so that every student in every class feels like today's class was the best class they've taken.

You pay attention to every detail to be sure everything is perfect. You even remind your staff to have a breath mint before they start each class.

You get to your school just a little bit earlier than usual to be sure that you can attend to any last minute details.

Just before the day starts, you remind your staff to make Mr. Norris feel welcome in your school. You remind them not to run at him the moment he walks in, but not wait so long to welcome him that he starts to wonder if anyone knows he's there. Remind them that since he's never visited your school, it might take him a few moments to feel comfortable there.

It's not frantic. You don't want him to feel that you're all totally on edge. You want him to get the sense that you're genuinely happy to see him but at the same time, you maintain a low key confidence that tells him that he has come to the best Martial Arts school in your city. When Mr. Norris walks in, he is completely impressed with you, your staff and your school.

*And of course, you know that Mr. Norris isn't really in your town. And he won't be training at your school today. But what would happen if you treated every day like the day that a very special guest was coming to your school? How great would your retention be if you put that extra preparation and energy into every class you teach? And what percentage of your prospects would enroll if you made that extra effort to make an exceptional first impression?*

Going the extra mile every day isn't easy, but it will make your school stand out from all the other schools in your city. It will clearly differentiate your program from all the other afterschool activities out there. And it will make your school a very popular place to train for kids, teens and adults.

KEYS TO GETTING YOUR STUDENTS TO TRAIN WITH YOU FOR 10 OR MORE YEARS

BELIEVE THEY WILL TRAIN WITH YOU FOR 10 YEARS.

This is essential. If you don't believe it, it won't happen. It might feel as if you're putting the cart before the horse by believing your students will train with you for ten or more years before it actually happens, but this is the first step. And it's absolutely necessary. So take the leap of faith and imprint this into your belief system.

PAY CLOSE ATTENTION TO YOUR INTERNAL RESISTANCE TO THIS.

Say out loud, "My students will train with me for ten years or more." If you're like most people, a skeptical voice in your head will quickly tell you all the reasons this won't happen. There can be all kinds of reasons why you might be skeptical of this. Listening to these objections will give you some ideas for things you might want to adjust. For example, one reason may be that they'll be bored long before then. This may be true now. But if you believe this is true, that's your signal to put extra effort into making every class fun, interesting and challenging (and perhaps give yourself a refresher course on disguising repetition along with thinking up some exciting new drills).

Be sure to separate your thoughts of resistance into things you can't address and things you can. Obviously, if someone starts your program when they're 14, there is a strong chance that you'll lose them four years later when they move away to college. There's not much you can do about that. But if you focus on students who start at eight or younger, or 22 and older, the reasons they might leave within ten years are more within your control.

GET YOUR STUDENTS OFF TO A GREAT START.

Here's the perfect formula for their first several weeks:

- Find out what they're hoping for and what their concerns are in your introduction. Develop a plan to give them more than what they're hoping for. Be sure to address their concerns quickly and thoroughly.

- Orchestrate their first class so that they LOVE the experience and can't wait to come back.

- By the end of their second week, they should feel completely comfortable with the instructor and the other students in the class.

- Make sure that they feel that their efforts and accomplishments are acknowledged.

- Find just the right moment to tell them that you can look ahead and see them as an awesome black belt in your program. They'll start sharing that vision and get excited about the prospect of actually earning their black belt. Then they will happily make a commitment to earning their black belt. Students realize that they love training at your school and parents are thrilled because you gave them exactly what they were hoping for and more. (This didn't happen by accident. See the first bullet in this set).

- Communication in their first several weeks is vital. The only way to know for sure if they're getting off to a great start is to get feedback. It's easy to make course corrections early before small concerns become major issues, but only if you know what they're thinking.

- Get them over their first obstacle. This can come in many different forms, but it's going to come. So be ready. And after they've overcome it, be sure to make them feel great about it. The next time they encounter an obstacle, they'll be ready to persevere through it.

BE SURE TO INVEST SIMILAR ENERGY INTO THE SATISFACTION OF THE PARENT.

Go out of your way to engage with parents. Compliment and appreciate their child. Every parent loves this!

MAKE YOUR SCHOOL A GENUINE COMMUNITY.

Starbucks refers to their stores as being their customers' third place. Home is their first place. Work or school is their second place. And, for you, your Martial Arts school is their third place. It's the place they love to be when they're not at home, school or work. Think about ways to make your school a social hub for your students and parents. While your Martial Arts program is always the core of what goes on at your school, your goal is to have your school be your students' favorite place to be.

NEVER UNDERESTIMATE THE POWER OF THE PERSONAL TOUCH.

Take a moment to look your students in the eye and tell them you're proud of them. Send handwritten Awesome Cards, birthday cards, etc.

*If they love coming to class...if they can't wait to come back...if they feel like they're an integral part of the school...if your school is their favorite place to be...if they feel acknowledged, appreciated and heard...if they have positive relationships with their instructor and their fellow students...then they'll never want to quit. And as long as the person paying feels that what they're getting is priceless, they'll do anything to keep coming back for more.*

# EPILOGUE: YOUR POWER TO CHANGE LIVES

Training in Martial Arts helps children and adults in nearly every aspect of their lives. It improves their health, fitness, athletic abilities, confidence, concentration, behavior at home and school, and performance in business.

To make an impact, we must all learn to become the very best teachers we possibly can. We must begin with the simple understanding of the important position we have taken on.

The single most important value that Martial Arts teachers can have is to believe in their students. I believe that you, as a Martial Arts instructor, have the power to improve the lives of children and adults in an epic way every day.

www.kovarsystems.com

Made in the USA
San Bernardino, CA
20 March 2016